The Complete Poetical Works of Edgar Allan Poe

By John H. Ingram
This Edition Edited by Anthony Uyl

Woodstock, Ontario, Canada 2018

The Complete Poetical Works of Edgar Allan Poe

The Complete Poetical Works of Edgar Allan Poe
By John H. Ingram
This Edition Edited by Anthony Uyl

The text of The Complete Poetical Works of Edgar Allan Poe is all in the Public Domain. The layout and Devoted Publishing logo are Copyright ©2018 Devoted Publishing. This edition is published by Devoted Publishing a division of 2165467 Ontario Inc.

**What kind of philosophies do you have?
Let us know!**

Visit our website: www.devotedpublishing.com
Contact us at: devotedpub@hotmail.com
Visit us on Facebook: @DevotedPublishing

Published in Woodstock, Ontario, Canada 2018.

For bulk educational rates, please contact us at the above email address.

ISBN: 978-1-77356-245-2

Table of Contents

PREFACE 5
MEMOIR OF EDGAR ALLAN POE 6
POEMS OF LATER LIFE 20
PREFACE 21
THE RAVEN 22
THE BELLS 25
ULALUME 28
TO HELEN 31
ANNABEL LEE 33
A VALENTINE 35
AN ENIGMA 36
TO MY MOTHER 37
FOR ANNIE 38
TO F-- 41
TO FRANCES S. OSGOOD. 42
ELDORADO 43
EULALIE 44
A DREAM WITHIN A DREAM 45
TO MARIE LOUISE (SHEW) 46
TO MARIE LOUISE (SHEW) 47
THE CITY IN THE SEA 48
THE SLEEPER 50
BRIDAL BALLAD 52
NOTES 53
POEMS OF MANHOOD 58
LENORE 58
TO ONE IN PARADISE 59
THE COLISEUM 60
THE HAUNTED PALACE 62
THE CONQUEROR WORM 64
SILENCE 66
DREAMLAND 67
TO ZANTE 69
HYMN 70
NOTES 71
SCENES FROM "POLITIAN" 73
AN UNPUBLISHED DRAMA 73
    Footnotes: 89
NOTE ON POLITIAN 90
POEMS OF YOUTH 94
INTRODUCTION TO POEMS--1831 94
SONNET--TO SCIENCE 99
    Footnotes: 99
AL AARAAF 100
    Footnotes: 109
TAMERLANE 112
TO HELEN 118
THE VALLEY OF UNREST 119
ISRAFEL 120
    Footnotes: 121
TO---- 122
TO---- 123
TO THE RIVER 124
SONG 125
SPIRITS OF THE DEAD 126
A DREAM 127
ROMANCE 128
FAIRYLAND 129
THE LAKE 131
EVENING STAR 132
IMITATION 133
"THE HAPPIEST DAY" 134
HYMN TO ARISTOGEITON AND HARMODIUS 135
DREAMS 136
    Footnotes: 136
"IN YOUTH I HAVE KNOWN ONE." . 137
    Footnotes: 138
A PÆAN 139
NOTES 141
DOUBTFUL POEMS 144
ALONE 144
TO ISADORE 145
THE VILLAGE STREET 147
THE FOREST REVERIE 149
NOTES 150

The Complete Poetical Works of Edgar Allan Poe

PROSE POEMS 151
THE ISLAND OF THE FAY 151
    Footnotes: 154
THE POWER OF WORDS 155
THE COLLOQUY OF MONOS AND UNA 159
    Footnotes: 165
THE CONVERSATION OF EIROS AND CHARMION 166
SHADOW--A PARABLE 171
SILENCE--A FABLE 173
ESSAYS 176
THE POETIC PRINCIPLE 176
THE PHILOSOPHY OF COMPOSITION 194
OLD ENGLISH POETRY 202
    Footnotes: 205

PREFACE

In placing before the public this collection of Edgar Poe's poetical works, it is requisite to point out in what respects it differs from, and is superior to, the numerous collections which have preceded it. Until recently, all editions, whether American or English, of Poe's poems have been 'verbatim' reprints of the first posthumous collection, published at New York in 1850.

In 1874 I began drawing attention to the fact that unknown and unreprinted poetry by Edgar Poe was in existence. Most, if not all, of the specimens issued in my articles have since been reprinted by different editors and publishers, but the present is the first occasion on which all the pieces referred to have been garnered into one sheaf. Besides the poems thus alluded to, this volume will be found to contain many additional pieces and extra stanzas, nowhere else published or included in Poe's works. Such verses have been gathered from printed or manuscript sources during a research extending over many years.

In addition to the new poetical matter included in this volume, attention should, also, be solicited on behalf of the notes, which will be found to contain much matter, interesting both from biographical and bibliographical points of view.

JOHN H. INGRAM.

MEMOIR OF EDGAR ALLAN POE.

During the last few years every incident in the life of Edgar Poe has been subjected to microscopic investigation. The result has not been altogether satisfactory. On the one hand, envy and prejudice have magnified every blemish of his character into crime, whilst on the other, blind admiration would depict him as far "too good for human nature's daily food." Let us endeavor to judge him impartially, granting that he was as a mortal subject to the ordinary weaknesses of mortality, but that he was tempted sorely, treated badly, and suffered deeply.

The poet's ancestry and parentage are chiefly interesting as explaining some of the complexities of his character. His father, David Poe, was of Anglo-Irish extraction. Educated for the Bar, he elected to abandon it for the stage. In one of his tours through the chief towns of the United States he met and married a young actress, Elizabeth Arnold, member of an English family distinguished for its musical talents. As an actress, Elizabeth Poe acquired some reputation, but became even better known for her domestic virtues. In those days the United States afforded little scope for dramatic energy, so it is not surprising to find that when her husband died, after a few years of married life, the young widow had a vain struggle to maintain herself and three little ones, William Henry, Edgar, and Rosalie. Before her premature death, in December, 1811, the poet's mother had been reduced to the dire necessity of living on the charity of her neighbors.

Edgar, the second child of David and Elizabeth Poe, was born at Boston, in the United States, on the 19th of January, 1809. Upon his mother's death at Richmond, Virginia, Edgar was adopted by a wealthy Scotch merchant, John Allan. Mr. Allan, who had married an American lady and settled in Virginia, was childless. He therefore took naturally to the brilliant and beautiful little boy, treated him as his son, and made him take his own surname. Edgar Allan, as he was now styled, after some elementary tuition in Richmond, was taken to England by his adopted parents, and, in 1816, placed at the Manor House School, Stoke-Newington.

Under the Rev. Dr. Bransby, the future poet spent a lustrum of his life neither unprofitably nor, apparently, ungenially. Dr. Bransby, who is himself so quaintly portrayed in Poe's tale of 'William Wilson', described "Edgar Allan," by which name only he knew the lad, as "a quick and clever boy," who "would have been a very good boy had he not been spoilt by his parents," meaning, of course, the Allans. They "allowed him an extravagant amount of pocket-money, which enabled him to get into all manner of mischief. Still I liked the boy," added the tutor, "but, poor fellow, his parents spoiled him."

Poe has described some aspects of his school days in his oft cited story of 'William Wilson'. Probably there is the usual amount of poetic exaggeration in these reminiscences, but they are almost the only record we have of that portion of his career and, therefore, apart from their literary merits, are on that account deeply interesting. The description of the sleepy old London suburb, as it was in those days, is remarkably accurate, but the revisions which the story of 'William Wilson' went through before it reached its present perfect state caused many of the author's details to deviate widely from their original correctness. His schoolhouse in the earliest draft was truthfully described as an "old, irregular, and cottage-built" dwelling, and so it remained until its destruction a few years ago.

The 'soi-disant' William Wilson, referring to those bygone happy days spent in the English academy, says,

> "The teeming brain of childhood requires no external world of incident to occupy or amuse it. The morning's awakening, the nightly summons to bed; the connings, the recitations, the periodical half-holidays and perambulations, the playground, with its broils, its pastimes, its intrigues--these, by a mental sorcery long forgotten, were made to involve a wilderness of sensation, a world of rich incident, a universe of varied emotion, of excitement the most passionate and spirit-stirring, 'Oh, le bon temps, que ce siècle de fer!'"

From this world of boyish imagination Poe was called to his adopted parents' home in the United States. He returned to America in 1821, and was speedily placed in an academy in Richmond, Virginia, in which city the Allans continued to reside. Already well grounded in the elementary processes of education, not without reputation on account of his European residence, handsome, proud, and regarded as the heir of a wealthy man, Poe must have been looked up to with no little respect by his fellow pupils. He speedily made himself a prominent position in the school, not only by his classical attainments, but by his athletic feats--accomplishments calculated to render him a leader among lads.

> "In the simple school athletics of those days, when a gymnasium had not been heard of, he was 'facile princeps',"

is the reminiscence of his fellow pupil, Colonel T. L. Preston. Poe he remembers as

> "a swift runner, a wonderful leaper, and, what was more rare, a boxer, with some slight training.... He would allow the strongest boy in the school to strike him with full force in the chest. He taught me the secret, and I imitated him, after my measure. It was to inflate the lungs to the uttermost, and at the moment of receiving the blow to exhale the air. It looked surprising, and was, indeed, a little rough; but with a good breast-bone, and some resolution, it was not difficult to stand it. For swimming he was noted, being in many of his athletic proclivities surprisingly like Byron in his youth."

In one of his feats Poe only came off second best.

> "A challenge to a foot race," says Colonel Preston, "had been passed between the two classical schools of the city; we selected Poe as our champion. The race came off one bright May morning at sunrise, in the Capitol Square. Historical truth compels me to add that on this occasion our school was beaten,

and we had to pay up our small bets. Poe ran well, but his competitor was a long-legged, Indian-looking fellow, who would have outstripped Atalanta without the help of the golden apples." "In our Latin exercises in school," continues the colonel, "Poe was among the first--not first without dispute. We had competitors who fairly disputed the palm, especially one, Nat Howard, afterwards known as one of the ripest scholars in Virginia, and distinguished also as a profound lawyer. If Howard was less brilliant than Poe, he was far more studious; for even then the germs of waywardness were developing in the nascent poet, and even then no inconsiderable portion of his time was given to versifying. But if I put Howard as a Latinist on a level with Poe, I do him full justice." "Poe," says the colonel, "was very fond of the Odes of Horace, and repeated them so often in my hearing that I learned by sound the words of many before I understood their meaning. In the lilting rhythm of the Sapphics and Iambics, his ear, as yet untutored in more complicated harmonies, took special delight. Two odes, in particular, have been humming in my ear all my life since, set to the tune of his recitation:

>   'Jam satis terris nivis atque dirce
>   Grandinis misit Pater, et rubente,'

And

>   'Non ebur neque aureum
>   Mea renidet in dono lacu ar,' etc.

"I remember that Poe was also a very fine French scholar. Yet, with all his superiorities, he was not the master spirit nor even the favorite of the school. I assign, from my recollection, this place to Howard. Poe, as I recall my impressions now, was self-willed, capricious, inclined to be imperious, and, though of generous impulses, not steadily kind, nor even amiable; and so what he would exact was refused to him. I add another thing which had its influence, I am sure. At the time of which I speak, Richmond was one of the most aristocratic cities on this side of the Atlantic.... A school is, of its nature, democratic; but still boys will unconsciously bear about the odor of their fathers' notions, good or bad. Of Edgar Poe," who had then resumed his parental cognomen, "it was known that his parents had been players, and that he was dependent upon the bounty that is bestowed upon an adopted son. All this had the effect of making the boys decline his leadership; and, on looking back on it since, I fancy it gave him a fierceness he would otherwise not have had."

This last paragraph of Colonel Preston's recollections cast a suggestive light upon the causes which rendered unhappy the lad's early life and tended to blight his prospective hopes. Although mixing with members of the best families of the province, and naturally endowed with hereditary and native pride,--fostered by the indulgence of wealth and the consciousness of intellectual superiority,--Edgar Poe was made to feel that his parentage was obscure, and that he himself was dependent upon the charity and caprice of an alien by blood. For many lads these things would have had but little meaning, but to one of Poe's proud temperament it must have been a source of constant torment, and all allusions to it gall and wormwood. And Mr. Allan was not the man to wean Poe from such festering fancies: as a rule he was proud of the handsome and talented boy, and indulged him in all that wealth could purchase, but at other times he treated him with contumely, and made him feel the bitterness of his position.

Still Poe did maintain his leading position among the scholars at that Virginian academy, and several still living have favored us with reminiscences of him. His feats in swimming to which Colonel Preston has alluded, are quite a feature of his youthful career. Colonel Mayo records one daring performance in natation which is thoroughly characteristic of the lad. One day in mid-winter, when standing on the banks of the James River, Poe dared his comrade into jumping in, in order to swim to a certain point with him. After floundering about in the nearly frozen stream for some time, they reached the piles upon which Mayo's Bridge was then supported, and there attempted to rest and try to gain the shore by climbing up the log abutment to the bridge. Upon reaching the bridge, however, they were dismayed to find that its plank flooring overlapped the abutment by several feet, and that it was impossible to ascend it. Nothing remained for them but to let go their slippery hold and swim back to the shore. Poe reached the bank in an exhausted and benumbed condition, whilst Mayo was rescued by a boat just as he was succumbing. On getting ashore Poe was seized with a violent attack of vomiting, and both lads were ill for several weeks.

Alluding to another quite famous swimming feat of his own, the poet remarked, "Any 'swimmer in the falls' in my days would have swum the Hellespont, and thought nothing of the matter. I swam from Ludlam's Wharf to Warwick (six miles), in a hot June sun, against one of the strongest tides ever known in the river. It would have been a feat comparatively easy to swim twenty miles in still water. I would not think much," Poe added in a strain of exaggeration not unusual with him, "of attempting to swim the British Channel from Dover to Calais." Colonel Mayo, who had tried to accompany him in this performance, had to stop on the way, and says that Poe, when he reached the goal, emerged from the water with neck, face, and back blistered. The facts of this feat, which was undertaken for a wager, having been questioned, Poe, ever intolerant of contradiction, obtained and published the affidavits of several gentlemen who had witnessed it. They also certified that Poe did not seem at all fatigued, and that he walked back to Richmond immediately after the performance.

The poet is generally remembered at this part of his career to have been slight in figure and person, but to have been well made, active, sinewy, and graceful. Despite the fact that he was thus noted among his schoolfellows and indulged at home, he does not appear to have been in sympathy with his surroundings. Already dowered with the "hate of hate, the scorn of scorn," he appears to have made foes both among those who envied him and those whom, in the pride of intellectuality, he treated with pugnacious contempt. Beneath the haughty exterior, however, was a warm and passionate heart, which only needed circumstance to call forth an almost fanatical intensity of affection. A well-authenticated instance of this is thus related by Mrs. Whitman:

"While at the academy in Richmond, he one day accompanied a schoolmate to his home, where he saw, for the first time, Mrs. Helen Stannard, *the mother of his young friend. This lady, on entering the room, took his hands and spoke some gentle and gracious words of welcome, which so penetrated the sensitive heart of the orphan boy as to deprive him of the power of speech, and for a time almost of consciousness itself. He returned home in a dream, with but one thought, one hope in life--to hear again the sweet and gracious words that had made the desolate world so beautiful to him, and filled his lonely heart with the oppression of a new joy. This lady afterwards became the confidant of all his boyish sorrows, and hers was the one redeeming influence that saved and guided him in the earlier days of his turbulent and passionate youth."*

When Edgar was unhappy at home, which, says his aunt, Mrs. Clemm, "was very often the case, he went to Mrs. Stannard for sympathy, for consolation, and for advice." Unfortunately, the sad fortune which so frequently thwarted his hopes ended this friendship. The lady was overwhelmed by a terrible calamity, and at the period when her guiding voice was most requisite, she fell a prey to mental alienation. She died, and was entombed in a neighboring cemetery, but her poor boyish admirer could not endure to think of her lying lonely and forsaken in her vaulted home, so he would leave the house at night and visit her tomb. When the nights were drear, "when the autumnal rains fell, and the winds wailed mournfully over the graves, he lingered longest, and came away most regretfully."

The memory of this lady, of this "one idolatrous and purely ideal love" of his boyhood, was cherished to the last. The name of Helen frequently recurs in his youthful verses, "The Pæan," now first included in his poetical works, refers to her; and to her he inscribed the classic and exquisitely beautiful stanzas beginning "Helen, thy beauty is to me."

Another important item to be noted in this epoch of his life is that he was already a poet. Among his schoolfellows he appears to have acquired some little reputation as a writer of satirical verses; but of his poetry, of that which, as he declared, had been with him "not a purpose, but a passion," he probably preserved the secret, especially as we know that at his adoptive home poesy was a forbidden thing. As early as 1821 he appears to have essayed various pieces, and some of these were ultimately included in his first volume. With Poe poetry was a personal matter--a channel through which the turbulent passions of his heart found an outlet. With feelings such as were his, it came to pass, as a matter of course, that the youthful poet fell in love. His first affair of the heart is, doubtless, reminiscently portrayed in what he says of his boyish ideal, Byron. This passion, he remarks, "if passion it can properly be called, was of the most thoroughly romantic, shadowy, and imaginative character. It was born of the hour, and of the youthful necessity to love. It had no peculiar regard to the person, or to the character, or to the reciprocating affection... Any maiden, not immediately and positively repulsive," he deems would have suited the occasion of frequent and unrestricted intercourse with such an imaginative and poetic youth. "The result," he deems, "was not merely natural, or merely probable; it was as inevitable as destiny itself."

Between the lines may be read the history of his own love. "The Egeria of his dreams--the Venus Aphrodite that sprang in full and supernal loveliness from the bright foam upon the storm-tormented ocean of his thoughts," was a little girl, Elmira Royster, who lived with her father in a house opposite to the Allans in Richmond. The young people met again and again, and the lady, who has only recently passed away, recalled Edgar as "a beautiful boy," passionately fond of music, enthusiastic and impulsive, but with prejudices already strongly developed. A certain amount of love-making took place between the young people, and Poe, with his usual passionate energy, ere he left home for the University had persuaded his fair inamorata to engage herself to him. Poe left home for the University of Virginia, Charlottesville, in the beginning of 1825. lie wrote frequently to Miss Royster, but her father did not approve of the affair, and, so the story runs, intercepted the correspondence, until it ceased. At seventeen, Elmira became the bride of a Mr. Shelton, and it was not until some time afterwards that Poe discovered how it was his passionate appeals had failed to elicit any response from the object of his youthful affection.

Poe's short university career was in many respects a repetition of his course at the Richmond Academy. He became noted at Charlottesville both for his athletic feats and his scholastic successes. He entered as a student on February 1,1826, and remained till the close of the second session in December of that year.

"He entered the schools of ancient and modern languages, attending the lectures on Latin, Greek, French, Spanish, and Italian. I was a member of the last three classes," says Mr. William Wertenbaker, the recently deceased librarian, "and can testify that he was tolerably regular in his attendance, and a successful student, having obtained distinction at the final examination in Latin and French, and this was at that time the highest honor a student could obtain. The present regulations in regard to degrees had not then been adopted. Under existing regulations, he would have graduated in the two languages above-named, and have been entitled to diplomas."

These statements of Poe's classmate are confirmed by Dr. Harrison, chairman of the Faculty, who remarks that the poet was a great favorite with his fellow-students, and was noted for the remarkable rapidity with which he prepared his recitations and for their accuracy, his translations from the modern languages being especially noteworthy.

Several of Poe's classmates at Charlottesville have testified to his "noble qualities" and other good endowments, but they remember that his "disposition was rather retiring, and that he had few intimate associates." Mr. Thomas Boiling, one of his fellow-students who has favored us with reminiscences of him, says:

"I was 'acquainted', with him, but that is about all. My impression was, and is, that no one could say that he 'knew' him. He wore a melancholy face always, and even his smile--for I do not ever remember to have seen him laugh--seemed to be forced. When he engaged sometimes with others in athletic exercises, in which, so far as high or long jumping, I believe he excelled all the rest, Poe, with the same ever sad face, appeared to participate in what was amusement to the others more as a task than sport."

Poe had no little talent for drawing, and Mr. John Willis states that the walls of his college rooms were covered with his crayon sketches, whilst Mr. Boiling mentions, in connection with the poet's artistic facility, some interesting incidents. The two young men had purchased copies of a handsomely-illustrated edition of Byron's poems, and upon visiting Poe a few days after this purchase, Mr. Bolling found him engaged in copying one of the engravings with crayon upon his dormitory ceiling. He continued to amuse himself in this way from time to time until he had filled all the space in his room with life-size figures which, it is remembered by those who saw them, were highly ornamental and well executed.

As Mr. Bolling talked with his associate, Poe would continue to scribble away with his pencil, as if writing, and when his visitor jestingly remonstrated with him on his want of politeness, he replied that he had been all attention, and proved that he had by suitable comment, assigning as a reason for his apparent want of courtesy that he was trying 'to divide his mind,' to carry on a conversation and write sensibly upon a totally different subject at the same time.

Mr. Wertenbaker, in his interesting reminiscences of the poet, says:

"As librarian I had frequent official intercourse with Poe, but it was at or near the close of the session before I met him in the social circle. After spending an evening together at a private house he invited me, on our return, into his room. It was a cold night in December, and his fire having gone pretty nearly out, by the aid of some tallow candles, and the fragments of a small table which he broke up for the purpose, he soon rekindled it, and by its comfortable blaze I spent a very pleasant hour with him. On this occasion he spoke with regret of the large amount of money he had wasted, and of the debts he had contracted during the session. If my memory be not at fault, he estimated his indebtedness at $2,000 and, though they were gaming debts, he was earnest and emphatic in the declaration that he was bound by honor to pay them at the earliest opportunity."

This appears to have been Poe's last night at the university. He left it never to return, yet, short as was his sojourn there, he left behind him such honorable memories that his 'alma mater' is now only too proud to enrol his name among her most respected sons. Poe's adopted father, however, did not regard his 'protégé's' collegiate career with equal pleasure: whatever view he may have entertained of the lad's scholastic successes, he resolutely refused to discharge the gambling debts which, like too many of his classmates, he had incurred. A violent altercation took place between Mr. Allan and the youth, and Poe hastily quitted the shelter of home to try and make his way in the world alone.

Taking with him such poems as he had ready, Poe made his way to Boston, and there looked up some of his mother's old theatrical friends. Whether he thought of adopting the stage as a profession, or whether he thought of getting their assistance towards helping him to put a drama of his own upon the stage,--that dream of all young authors,--is now unknown. He appears to have wandered about for some time, and by some means or the other succeeded in getting a little volume of poems printed "for private circulation only." This was towards the end of 1827, when he was nearing nineteen. Doubtless Poe expected to dispose of his volume by subscription among his friends, but copies did not go off, and ultimately the book was suppressed, and the remainder of the edition, for "reasons of a private nature," destroyed.

What happened to the young poet, and how he contrived to exist for the next year or so, is a mystery still unsolved. It has always been believed that he found his way to Europe and met with some curious adventures there, and Poe himself certainly alleged that such was the case. Numbers of mythical stories have been invented to account for this chasm in the poet's life, and most of them self-evidently fabulous. In a recent biography of Poe an attempt had been made to prove that he enlisted in the army under an assumed name, and served for about eighteen months in the artillery in a highly creditable manner, receiving an honorable discharge at the instance of Mr. Allan. This account is plausible, but will need further explanation of its many discrepancies of dates, and verification of the different documents cited in proof of it, before the public can receive it as fact. So many fables have been published about Poe, and even many fictitious documents quoted, that it behoves the unprejudiced to be wary in accepting any new statements concerning him that are not thoroughly authenticated.

On the 28th February, 1829, Mrs. Allan died, and with her death the final thread that had bound Poe to her husband was broken. The adopted son arrived too late to take a last farewell of her whose influence had given the Allan residence its only claim upon the poet's heart. A kind of truce was patched up over the grave of the deceased lady, but, for the future, Poe found that home was home no longer.

Again the young man turned to poetry, not only as a solace but as a means of earning a livelihood. Again he printed a little volume of poems, which included his longest piece, "Al Aaraaf," and several others now deemed classic. The book was a great advance upon his previous collection, but failed to obtain any amount of public praise or personal profit for its author.

Feeling the difficulty of living by literature at the same time that he saw he might have to rely largely upon his own exertions for a livelihood, Poe expressed a wish to enter the army. After no little difficulty a cadetship was obtained for him at the West Point Military Academy, a military school in many respects equal to the best in Europe for the education of officers for the army. At the time Poe entered the Academy it possessed anything but an attractive character, the discipline having been of the most severe character, and the accommodation in many respects unsuitable for growing lads.

The poet appears to have entered upon this new course of life with his usual enthusiasm, and for a time to have borne the rigid rules of the place with unusual steadiness. He entered the institution on the 1st July, 1830, and by the following March had been expelled for determined disobedience. Whatever view may be taken of Poe's conduct upon this occasion, it must be seen that the expulsion from West Point was of his own seeking. Highly-colored pictures have been drawn of his eccentric behavior at the Academy, but the fact remains that he wilfully, or at any rate purposely, flung away his cadetship. It is surmised with plausibility that the second marriage of Mr. Allan, and his expressed intention of withdrawing his help and of not endowing or bequeathing this adopted son any of his property, was the mainspring of Poe's action. Believing it impossible to continue without aid in a profession so expensive as was a military life, he determined to relinquish it and return to his long cherished attempt to become an author.

Expelled from the institution that afforded board and shelter, and discarded by his former protector, the unfortunate and penniless young man yet a third time attempted to get a start in the world of letters by means of a volume of poetry. If it be true, as alleged, that several of his brother cadets aided his efforts by subscribing for his little work, there is some possibility that a few dollars rewarded this latest venture. Whatever may have resulted from the alleged aid, it is certain that in a short time after leaving the Military Academy Poe was reduced to sad straits. He disappeared for nearly two years from public notice, and how he lived during that period has never been satisfactorily explained. In 1833 he returns to history in the character of a winner of a hundred-dollar award offered by a newspaper for the best story.

The prize was unanimously adjudged to Poe by the adjudicators, and Mr. Kennedy, an author of some little repute, having become interested by the young man's evident genius, generously assisted him towards obtaining a livelihood by literary labor. Through his new friend's introduction to the proprietor of the 'Southern Literary Messenger', a moribund magazine published at irregular intervals, Poe became first a paid contributor, and eventually the editor of the publication, which ultimately he rendered one of the most respected and profitable periodicals of the day. This success was entirely due to the brilliancy and power of Poe's own contributions to the magazine.

In March, 1834, Mr. Allan died, and if our poet had maintained any hopes of further assistance from him, all doubt was settled by the will, by which the whole property of the deceased was left to his second wife and her three sons. Poe was not named.

On the 6th May, 1836, Poe, who now had nothing but his pen to trust to, married his cousin, Virginia Clemm, a child of only fourteen, and with her mother as housekeeper, started a home of his own. In the meantime his various writings in the 'Messenger' began to attract attention and to extend his reputation into literary circles, but beyond his editorial salary of about $520 brought him no pecuniary reward.

In January, 1837, for reasons never thoroughly explained, Poe severed his connection with the 'Messenger', and moved with all his household goods from Richmond to New York. Southern friends state that Poe was desirous of either being admitted into partnership with his employer, or of being allowed a larger share of the profits which his own labors procured. In New York his earnings seem to have been small and irregular, his most important work having been a republication from the 'Messenger' in book form of his Defoe-like romance entitled 'Arthur Gordon Pym'. The truthful air of "The Narrative," as well as its other merits, excited public curiosity both in England and America; but Poe's remuneration does not appear to have been proportionate to its success, nor did he receive anything from the numerous European editions the work rapidly passed through.

In 1838 Poe was induced by a literary friend to break up his New York home and remove with his wife and aunt (her mother) to Philadelphia. The Quaker city was at that time quite a hotbed for magazine projects, and among the many new periodicals Poe was enabled to earn some kind of a living. To Burton's 'Gentleman's Magazine' for 1837 he had contributed a few articles, but in 1840 he arranged with its proprietor to take up the editorship. Poe had long sought to start a magazine of his own, and it was probably with a view to such an eventuality that one of his conditions for accepting the editorship of the 'Gentleman's Magazine' was that his name should appear upon the title-page.

Poe worked hard at the 'Gentleman's' for some time, contributing to its columns much of his best work; ultimately, however, he came to loggerheads with its proprietor, Burton, who disposed of the magazine to a Mr. Graham, a rival publisher. At this period Poe collected into two volumes, and got them published as 'Tales of the Grotesque and Arabesques', twenty-five of his stories, but he never received any remuneration, save a few copies of the volumes, for the work. For some time the poet strove most earnestly to start a magazine of his own, but all his efforts failed owing to his want of capital.

The purchaser of Burton's magazine, having amalgamated it with another, issued the two under the title of 'Graham's Magazine'. Poe became a contributor to the new venture, and in November of the year 1840 consented to assume the post of editor.

Under Poe's management, assisted by the liberality of Mr. Graham, 'Graham's Magazine' became a grand success. To its pages Poe contributed some of his finest and most popular tales, and attracted to the publication the pens of many of the best contemporary authors. The public was not slow in showing its appreciation of 'pabulum' put before it, and, so its directors averred, in less than two years the circulation rose from five to fifty-two thousand copies.

A great deal of this success was due to Poe's weird and wonderful stories; still more, perhaps, to his trenchant critiques and his startling theories anent cryptology. As regards the tales now issued in 'Graham's', attention may especially be drawn to the world-famed "Murders in the Rue Morgue," the first of a series--'"une espèce de trilogie,"' as Baudelaire styles them--illustrative of an analytic phase of Poe's peculiar mind. This 'trilogie' of tales, of which the later two were "The Purloined Letter" and "The Mystery of Marie Roget," was avowedly written to prove the capability of solving the puzzling riddles of life by identifying another person's mind by our own. By trying to follow the processes by which a person would reason out a certain thing, Poe propounded the theory that another person might ultimately arrive, as it were, at that person's conclusions, indeed, penetrate the innermost arcanum of his brain and read his most secret thoughts. Whilst the public was still pondering over the startling proposition, and enjoying perusal of its apparent proofs, Poe still further increased his popularity and drew attention to his works by putting forward the attractive but less dangerous theorem that "human ingenuity could not construct a cipher which human ingenuity could not solve."

This cryptographic assertion was made in connection with what the public deemed a challenge, and Poe was inundated with ciphers more or less abstruse, demanding solution. In the correspondence which ensued in 'Graham's Magazine' and other publications, Poe was universally acknowledged to have proved his case, so far as his own personal ability to unriddle such mysteries was concerned. Although he had never offered to undertake such a task, he triumphantly solved every cryptogram sent to him, with one exception, and that exception he proved conclusively was only an imposture, for which no solution was possible.

The outcome of this exhaustive and unprofitable labor was the fascinating story of "The Gold Bug," a story in which the discovery of hidden treasure is brought about by the unriddling of an intricate cipher.

The year 1841 may be deemed the brightest of Poe's checkered career. On every side acknowledged to be a new and brilliant literary light, chief editor of a powerful magazine, admired, feared, and envied, with a reputation already spreading rapidly in Europe as well as in his native continent, the poet might well have hoped for prosperity and happiness. But dark cankers were gnawing his heart. His pecuniary position was still embarrassing. His writings, which were the result of slow and careful labor, were poorly paid, and his remuneration as joint editor of 'Graham's' was small. He was not permitted to have undivided control, and but a slight share of the profits of the magazine he had rendered world-famous, whilst a fearful domestic calamity wrecked all his hopes, and caused him to resort to that refuge of the broken-hearted--to that drink which finally destroyed his prospects and his life.

Edgar Poe's own account of this terrible malady and its cause was made towards the end of his career. Its truth has never been disproved, and in its most important points it has been thoroughly substantiated. To a correspondent he writes in January 1848:

"You say, 'Can you hint to me what was "that terrible evil" which caused the "irregularities" so profoundly lamented?' Yes, I can do more than hint. This evil was the greatest which can befall a man. Six years ago, a wife whom I loved as no man ever loved before, ruptured a blood-vessel in singing. Her life was despaired of. I took leave of her forever, and underwent all the agonies of her death. She recovered partially, and I again hoped. At the end of a year, the vessel broke again. I went through precisely the same scene.... Then again--again--and even once again at varying intervals. Each time I felt all the agonies of her death--and at each accession of the disorder I loved her more dearly and clung to her life with more desperate pertinacity. But I am constitutionally sensitive--nervous in a very unusual degree. I became insane, with long intervals of horrible sanity. During these fits of absolute unconsciousness, I drank--God only knows how often or how much. As a matter of course, my enemies referred the insanity to the drink rather than the drink to the insanity. I had, indeed, nearly abandoned all hope of a permanent cure, when I found one in the death of my wife. This I can and do endure as becomes a man. It was the horrible never-ending oscillation between hope and despair which I could not longer have endured, without total loss of reason."

The poet at this period was residing in a small but elegant little home, superintended by his ever-faithful guardian, his wife's mother--his own aunt, Mrs. Clemm, the lady whom he so gratefully addressed in after years in the well-known sonnet, as "more than mother unto me." But a change came o'er the spirit of his dream! His severance from 'Graham's', owing to we know not what causes, took place, and his fragile schemes of happiness faded as fast as the sunset. His means melted away, and he became unfitted by mental trouble and ill-health to earn more. The terrible straits to which he and his unfortunate beloved ones were reduced may be comprehended after perusal of these words from Mr. A. B. Harris's reminiscences.

Referring to the poet's residence in Spring Gardens, Philadelphia, this writer says:

"It was during their stay there that Mrs. Poe, while singing one evening, ruptured a blood-vessel, and after that she suffered a hundred deaths. She could not bear the slightest exposure, and needed the utmost care; and all those conveniences as to apartment and surroundings which are so important in the case of an invalid were almost matters of life and death to her. And yet the room where she lay for weeks, hardly able to breathe, except as she was

fanned, was a little narrow place, with the ceiling so low over the narrow bed that her head almost touched it. But no one dared to speak, Mr. Poe was so sensitive and irritable; 'quick as steel and flint,' said one who knew him in those days. And he would not allow a word about the danger of her dying: the mention of it drove him wild."

Is it to be wondered at, should it not indeed be forgiven him, if, impelled by the anxieties and privations at home, the unfortunate poet, driven to the brink of madness, plunged still deeper into the Slough of Despond? Unable to provide for the pressing necessities of his beloved wife, the distracted man

"would steal out of the house at night, and go off and wander about the street for hours, proud, heartsick, despairing, not knowing which way to turn, or what to do, while Mrs. Clemm would endure the anxiety at home as long as she could, and then start off in search of him."

During his calmer moments Poe exerted all his efforts to proceed with his literary labors. He continued to contribute to 'Graham's Magazine,' the proprietor of which periodical remained his friend to the end of his life, and also to some other leading publications of Philadelphia and New York. A suggestion having been made to him by N. P. Willis, of the latter city, he determined to once more wander back to it, as he found it impossible to live upon his literary earnings where he was.

Accordingly, about the middle of 1845, Poe removed to New York, and shortly afterwards was engaged by Willis and his partner Morris as sub-editor on the 'Evening Mirror'. He was, says Willis,

"employed by us for several months as critic and subeditor.... He resided with his wife and mother at Fordham, a few miles out of town, but was at his desk in the office from nine in the morning till the evening paper went to press. With the highest admiration for his genius, and a willingness to let it atone for more than ordinary irregularity, we were led by common report to expect a very capricious attention to his duties, and occasionally a scene of violence and difficulty. Time went on, however, and he was invariably punctual and industrious. With his pale, beautiful, and intellectual face, as a reminder of what genius was in him, it was impossible, of course, not to treat him always with deferential courtsey.... With a prospect of taking the lead in another periodical, he at last voluntarily gave up his employment with us."

A few weeks before Poe relinquished his laborious and ill-paid work on the 'Evening Mirror', his marvellous poem of "The Raven" was published. The effect was magical. Never before, nor, indeed, ever since, has a single short poem produced such a great and immediate enthusiasm. It did more to render its author famous than all his other writings put together. It made him the literary lion of the season; called into existence innumerable parodies; was translated into various languages, and, indeed, created quite a literature of its own. Poe was naturally delighted with the success his poem had attained, and from time to time read it in his musical manner in public halls or at literary receptions. Nevertheless he affected to regard it as a work of art only, and wrote his essay entitled the "Philosophy of Composition," to prove that it was merely a mechanical production made in accordance with certain set rules.

Although our poet's reputation was now well established, he found it still a difficult matter to live by his pen. Even when in good health, he wrote slowly and with fastidious care, and when his work was done had great difficulty in getting publishers to accept it. Since his death it has been proved that many months often elapsed before he could get either his most admired poems or tales published.

Poe left the 'Evening Mirror' in order to take part in the 'Broadway Journal', wherein he re-issued from time to time nearly the whole of his prose and poetry. Ultimately he acquired possession of this periodical, but, having no funds to carry it on, after a few months of heartbreaking labor he had to relinquish it. Exhausted in body and mind, the unfortunate man now retreated with his dying wife and her mother to a quaint little cottage at Fordham, outside New York. Here after a time the unfortunate household was reduced to the utmost need, not even having wherewith to purchase the necessities of life. At this dire moment, some friendly hand, much to the indignation and dismay of Poe himself, made an appeal to the public on behalf of the hapless family.

The appeal had the desired effect. Old friends and new came to the rescue, and, thanks to them, and especially to Mrs. Shew, the "Marie Louise" of Poe's later poems, his wife's dying moments were soothed, and the poet's own immediate wants provided for. In January, 1846, Virginia Poe died; and for some time after her death the poet remained in an apathetic stupor, and, indeed, it may be truly said that never again did his mental faculties appear to regain their former power.

For another year or so Poe lived quietly at Fordham, guarded by the watchful care of Mrs. Clemm,--writing little, but thinking out his philosophical prose poem of "Eureka," which he deemed the crowning work of his life. His life was as abstemious and regular as his means were small. Gradually, however, as intercourse with fellow literati re-aroused his dormant energies, he began to meditate a fresh start in the world. His old and never thoroughly abandoned project of starting a magazine of his own, for the enunciation of his own views on literature, now absorbed all his thoughts. In order to get the necessary funds for establishing his publication on a solid footing, he determined to give a series of lectures in various parts of the States.

His re-entry into public life only involved him in a series of misfortunes. At one time he was engaged to be married to Mrs. Whitman, a widow lady of considerable intellectual and literary attainments; but, after several incidents of a highly romantic character, the match was broken off. In 1849 Poe revisited the South, and, amid the scenes and friends of his early life, passed some not altogether unpleasing time. At Richmond, Virginia, he again met his first love, Elmira, now a wealthy widow, and, after a short renewed acquaintance, was once more engaged to marry her. But misfortune continued to dog his steps.

A publishing affair recalled him to New York. He left Richmond by boat for Baltimore, at which city he arrived on the 3d October, and handed his trunk to a porter to carry to the train for Philadelphia. What now happened has never been clearly explained. Previous to starting on his journey, Poe had complained of indisposition,--of chilliness and of exhaustion,--and it is not improbable that an increase or continuance of these symptoms had tempted him to drink, or to resort to some of those narcotics he is known to have indulged in towards the close of his life. Whatever the cause of his delay, the consequences were fatal. Whilst in a state of temporary mania or insensibility, he fell into the hands of a band of ruffians, who were scouring the streets in search of accomplices or victims. What followed is given on undoubted authority.

His captors carried the unfortunate poet into an electioneering den, where they drugged him with whisky. It was election day for a member of Congress, and Poe with other victims, was dragged from polling station to station, and forced to vote the ticket placed in his hand. Incredible as it may appear, the superintending officials of those days registered the proffered vote, quite regardless of the condition of the person personifying a voter. The election over, the dying poet was left in the streets to perish, but, being found ere life was extinct, he was carried to the Washington University Hospital, where he expired on the 7th of October, 1849, in the forty-first year of his age.

Edgar Poe was buried in the family grave of his grandfather, General Poe, in the presence of a few friends and relatives. On the 17th November, 1875, his remains were removed from their first resting-place and, in the presence of a large number of people, were placed under a marble monument subscribed for by some of his many admirers. His wife's body has recently been placed by his side.

The story of that "fitful fever" which constituted the life of Edgar Poe leaves upon the reader's mind the conviction that he was, indeed, truly typified by that:

"Unhappy master, whom unmerciful disaster
Followed fast and followed faster till his songs one burden bore--
Till the dirges of his hope that melancholy burden bore
    Of 'Never--nevermore.'"

JOHN H. INGRAM.

POEMS OF LATER LIFE

To the Noblest of her Sex—to the Author of "The Drama of Exile"—to Miss Elizabeth Barrett Barrett, of England, I Dedicate this Volume with the Most Enthusiastic Admiration and with the Most Sincere Esteem

1845 E.A.P.

PREFACE

These trifles are collected and republished chiefly with a view to their redemption from the many improvements to which they have been subjected while going at random the "rounds of the press." I am naturally anxious that what I have written should circulate as I wrote it, if it circulate at all. In defence of my own taste, nevertheless, it is incumbent upon me to say that I think nothing in this volume of much value to the public, or very creditable to myself. Events not to be controlled have prevented me from making, at any time, any serious effort in what, under happier circumstances, would have been the field of my choice. With me poetry has been not a purpose, but a passion; and the passions should be held in reverence: they must not--they cannot at will be excited, with an eye to the paltry compensations, or the more paltry commendations, of mankind.

1845. E.A.P.

THE RAVEN

Once upon a midnight dreary, while I pondered, weak and weary,
Over many a quaint and curious volume of forgotten lore--
While I nodded, nearly napping, suddenly there came a tapping,
As of some one gently rapping--rapping at my chamber door.
"'Tis some visitor," I muttered, "tapping at my chamber door--
    Only this and nothing more."

Ah, distinctly I remember, it was in the bleak December,
And each separate dying ember wrought its ghost upon the floor.
Eagerly I wished the morrow;--vainly I had sought to borrow
From my books surcease of sorrow--sorrow for the lost Lenore--
For the rare and radiant maiden whom the angels name Lenore--
    Nameless here for evermore.

And the silken sad uncertain rustling of each purple curtain
Thrilled me--filled me with fantastic terrors never felt before;
So that now, to still the beating of my heart, I stood repeating
"'Tis some visitor entreating entrance at my chamber door--
Some late visitor entreating entrance at my chamber door;--
    This it is and nothing more."

Presently my soul grew stronger; hesitating then no longer,
"Sir," said I, "or Madam, truly your forgiveness I implore;
But the fact is I was napping, and so gently you came rapping,
And so faintly you came tapping--tapping at my chamber door,
That I scarce was sure I heard you"--here I opened wide the door:--
    Darkness there and nothing more.

Deep into that darkness peering, long I stood there wondering, fearing,
Doubting, dreaming dreams no mortal ever dared to dream before;
But the silence was unbroken, and the darkness gave no token,
And the only word there spoken was the whispered word, "Lenore!"
This I whispered, and an echo murmured back the word, "Lenore!"
    Merely this and nothing more.

Back into the chamber turning, all my soul within me burning,
Soon I heard again a tapping, somewhat louder than before.
"Surely," said I, "surely that is something at my window lattice;
Let me see, then, what thereat is, and this mystery explore--
Let my heart be still a moment, and this mystery explore;--
    'Tis the wind and nothing more."

Edgar Allan Poe

Open here I flung the shutter, when, with many a flirt and flutter,
In there stepped a stately Raven of the saintly days of yore;
Not the least obeisance made he: not an instant stopped or stayed he;
But, with mien of lord or lady, perched above my chamber door--
Perched upon a bust of Pallas just above my chamber door--
    Perched, and sat, and nothing more.

Then this ebony bird beguiling my sad fancy into smiling,
By the grave and stern decorum of the countenance it wore,
"Though thy crest be shorn and shaven, thou," I said, "art sure no craven,
Ghastly grim and ancient Raven wandering from the Nightly shore--
Tell me what thy lordly name is on the Night's Plutonian shore!"
    Quoth the Raven, "Nevermore."

Much I marvelled this ungainly fowl to hear discourse so plainly,
Though its answer little meaning--little relevancy bore;
For we cannot help agreeing that no living human being
Ever yet was blessed with seeing bird above his chamber door--
Bird or beast upon the sculptured bust above his chamber door,
    With such name as "Nevermore."

But the Raven, sitting lonely on that placid bust, spoke only
That one word, as if his soul in that one word he did outpour.
Nothing further then he uttered--not a feather then he fluttered--
Till I scarcely more than muttered, "Other friends have flown before--
On the morrow he will leave me, as my hopes have flown before."
    Then the bird said, "Nevermore."

Startled at the stillness broken by reply so aptly spoken,
"Doubtless," said I, "what it utters is its only stock and store,
Caught from some unhappy master whom unmerciful Disaster
Followed fast and followed faster till his songs one burden bore--
Till the dirges of his Hope the melancholy burden bore
    Of 'Never--nevermore.'"

But the Raven still beguiling all my sad soul into smiling,
Straight I wheeled a cushioned seat in front of bird and bust and door;
Then, upon the velvet sinking, I betook myself to linking
Fancy unto fancy, thinking what this ominous bird of yore--
What this grim, ungainly, ghastly, gaunt, and ominous bird of yore
    Meant in croaking "Nevermore."

This I sat engaged in guessing, but no syllable expressing
To the fowl whose fiery eyes now burned into my bosom's core;
This and more I sat divining, with my head at ease reclining
On the cushion's velvet lining that the lamp-light gloated o'er,
But whose velvet violet lining with the lamp-light gloating o'er,
    She shall press, ah, nevermore!

Then, methought, the air grew denser, perfumed from an unseen censer
Swung by Seraphim whose foot-falls tinkled on the tufted floor.
"Wretch," I cried, "thy God hath lent thee--by these angels he hath sent thee
Respite--respite aad nepenthé from thy memories of Lenore!
Quaff, oh quaff this kind nepenthé, and forget this lost Lenore!"
    Quoth the Raven, "Nevermore."

"Prophet!" said I, "thing of evil!--prophet still, if bird or devil!--
Whether Tempter sent, or whether tempest tossed thee here ashore,
Desolate yet all undaunted, on this desert land enchanted--
On this home by Horror haunted--tell me truly, I implore--
Is there--is there balm in Gilead?--tell me--tell me, I implore!"
    Quoth the Raven, "Nevermore."

"Prophet!" said I, "thing of evil!--prophet still, if bird or devil!
By that Heaven that bends above us--by that God we both adore--
Tell this soul with sorrow laden if, within the distant Aidenn,
It shall clasp a sainted maiden whom the angels name Lenore--
Clasp a rare and radiant maiden whom the angels name Lenore."
    Quoth the Raven, "Nevermore."

"Be that word our sign of parting, bird or fiend!" I shrieked, upstarting--
"Get thee back into the tempest and the Night's Plutonian shore!
Leave no black plume as a token of that lie thy soul hath spoken!
Leave my loneliness unbroken!--quit the bust above my door!
Take thy beak from out my heart, and take thy form from off my door!"
    Quoth the Raven, "Nevermore."

And the Raven, never flitting, still is sitting, still is sitting
On the pallid bust of Pallas just above my chamber door;
And his eyes have all the seeming of a demon's that is dreaming,
And the lamp-light o'er him streaming throws his shadow on the floor;
And my soul from out that shadow that lies floating on the floor
    Shall be lifted--nevermore!

    Published, 1845.

Edgar Allan Poe

THE BELLS

I.

Hear the sledges with the bells--
Silver bells!
What a world of merriment their melody foretells!
How they tinkle, tinkle, tinkle,
In their icy air of night!
While the stars, that oversprinkle
All the heavens, seem to twinkle
With a crystalline delight;
Keeping time, time, time,
In a sort of Runic rhyme,
To the tintinnabulation that so musically wells
From the bells, bells, bells, bells,
Bells, bells, bells--
From the jingling and the tinkling of the bells.

II.

Hear the mellow wedding bells,
Golden bells!
What a world of happiness their harmony foretells!
Through the balmy air of night
How they ring out their delight!
From the molten golden-notes,
And all in tune,
What a liquid ditty floats
To the turtle-dove that listens, while she gloats
On the moon!
Oh, from out the sounding cells,
What a gush of euphony voluminously wells!
How it swells!
How it dwells
On the future! how it tells
Of the rapture that impels
To the swinging and the ringing
Of the bells, bells, bells,
Of the bells, bells, bells, bells,
Bells, bells, bells--
To the rhyming and the chiming of the bells!

III.

Hear the loud alarum bells--
Brazen bells!
What a tale of terror now their turbulency tells!
In the startled ear of night
How they scream out their affright!
Too much horrified to speak,
They can only shriek, shriek,
Out of tune,
In a clamorous appealing to the mercy of the fire,
In a mad expostulation with the deaf and frantic fire
Leaping higher, higher, higher,
With a desperate desire,
And a resolute endeavor
Now--now to sit or never,
By the side of the pale-faced moon.
Oh, the bells, bells, bells!
What a tale their terror tells
Of Despair!
How they clang, and clash, and roar!
What a horror they outpour
On the bosom of the palpitating air!
Yet the ear it fully knows,
By the twanging,
And the clanging,
How the danger ebbs and flows;
Yet the ear distinctly tells,
In the jangling,
And the wrangling,
How the danger sinks and swells,
By the sinking or the swelling in the anger of the bells--
Of the bells--
Of the bells, bells, bells, bells,
Bells, bells, bells--
In the clamor and the clangor of the bells!

IV.

Hear the tolling of the bells--
Iron bells!
What a world of solemn thought their monody compels!
In the silence of the night,
How we shiver with affright
At the melancholy menace of their tone!
For every sound that floats
From the rust within their throats
    Is a groan.
And the people--ah, the people--
They that dwell up in the steeple.

      All alone,
And who toiling, toiling, toiling,
    In that muffled monotone,
Feel a glory in so rolling
      On the human heart a stone--
They are neither man nor woman--
They are neither brute nor human--
     They are Ghouls:
And their king it is who tolls;
And he rolls, rolls, rolls,
        Rolls
A pæan from the bells!
And his merry bosom swells
With the pæan of the bells!
And he dances, and he yells;
Keeping time, time, time,
In a sort of Runic rhyme,
To the pæan of the bells--
    Of the bells:
Keeping time, time, time,
In a sort of Runic rhyme,
    To the throbbing of the bells--
Of the bells, bells, bells--
    To the sobbing of the bells;
Keeping time, time, time,
    As he knells, knells, knells,
In a happy Runic rhyme,
To the rolling of the bells--
Of the bells, bells, bells--
To the tolling of the bells,
Of the bells, bells, bells, bells,
    Bells, bells, bells--
To the moaning and the groaning of the bells.

   1849.

ULALUME

The skies they were ashen and sober;
    The leaves they were crisped and sere--
    The leaves they were withering and sere;
It was night in the lonesome October
    Of my most immemorial year;
It was hard by the dim lake of Auber,
    In the misty mid region of Weir--
It was down by the dank tarn of Auber,
    In the ghoul-haunted woodland of Weir.

Here once, through an alley Titanic.
    Of cypress, I roamed with my Soul--
    Of cypress, with Psyche, my Soul.
These were days when my heart was volcanic
    As the scoriac rivers that roll--
    As the lavas that restlessly roll
Their sulphurous currents down Yaanek
    In the ultimate climes of the pole--
That groan as they roll down Mount Yaanek
    In the realms of the boreal pole.

Our talk had been serious and sober,
    But our thoughts they were palsied and sere--
    Our memories were treacherous and sere--
For we knew not the month was October,
And we marked not the night of the year--
    (Ah, night of all nights in the year!)
We noted not the dim lake of Auber--
    (Though once we had journeyed down here)--
Remembered not the dank tarn of Auber,
    Nor the ghoul-haunted woodland of Weir.

And now as the night was senescent
    And star-dials pointed to morn--
    As the sun-dials hinted of morn--
At the end of our path a liquescent
    And nebulous lustre was born,
Out of which a miraculous crescent
    Arose with a duplicate horn--
Astarte's bediamonded crescent
    Distinct with its duplicate horn.

And I said--"She is warmer than Dian:
    She rolls through an ether of sighs--
    She revels in a region of sighs:
She has seen that the tears are not dry on
    These cheeks, where the worm never dies,
And has come past the stars of the Lion
    To point us the path to the skies--
    To the Lethean peace of the skies--
Come up, in despite of the Lion,
    To shine on us with her bright eyes--
Come up through the lair of the Lion,
    With love in her luminous eyes."

But Psyche, uplifting her finger,
    Said--"Sadly this star I mistrust--
    Her pallor I strangely mistrust:--
Oh, hasten!--oh, let us not linger!
    Oh, fly!--let us fly!--for we must."
In terror she spoke, letting sink her
    Wings till they trailed in the dust--
In agony sobbed, letting sink her
    Plumes till they trailed in the dust--
    Till they sorrowfully trailed in the dust.

I replied--"This is nothing but dreaming:
    Let us on by this tremulous light!
    Let us bathe in this crystalline light!
Its Sibyllic splendor is beaming
    With Hope and in Beauty to-night:--
    See!--it flickers up the sky through the night!
Ah, we safely may trust to its gleaming,
    And be sure it will lead us aright--
We safely may trust to a gleaming
    That cannot but guide us aright,
    Since it flickers up to Heaven through the night."

Thus I pacified Psyche and kissed her,
    And tempted her out of her gloom--
    And conquered her scruples and gloom;
And we passed to the end of a vista,
    But were stopped by the door of a tomb--
    By the door of a legended tomb;
And I said--"What is written, sweet sister,
    On the door of this legended tomb?"
    She replied--"Ulalume--Ulalume--
    'Tis the vault of thy lost Ulalume!"

Then my heart it grew ashen and sober
    As the leaves that were crisped and sere--
    As the leaves that were withering and sere;

And I cried--"It was surely October
    On this very night of last year
    That I journeyed--I journeyed down here--
    That I brought a dread burden down here!
    On this night of all nights in the year,
    Ah, what demon has tempted me here?
Well I know, now, this dim lake of Auber--
    This misty mid region of Weir--
Well I know, now, this dank tarn of Auber,--
    This ghoul-haunted woodland of Weir."

1847.

Edgar Allan Poe

TO HELEN

I saw thee once--once only--years ago:
I must not say how many--but not many.
It was a July midnight; and from out
A full-orbed moon, that, like thine own soul, soaring,
Sought a precipitate pathway up through heaven,
There fell a silvery-silken veil of light,
With quietude, and sultriness and slumber,
Upon the upturn'd faces of a thousand
Roses that grew in an enchanted garden,
Where no wind dared to stir, unless on tiptoe--
Fell on the upturn'd faces of these roses
That gave out, in return for the love-light,
Their odorous souls in an ecstatic death--
Fell on the upturn'd faces of these roses
That smiled and died in this parterre, enchanted
By thee, and by the poetry of thy presence.

Clad all in white, upon a violet bank
I saw thee half-reclining; while the moon
Fell on the upturn'd faces of the roses,
And on thine own, upturn'd--alas, in sorrow!

Was it not Fate, that, on this July midnight--
Was it not Fate (whose name is also Sorrow),
That bade me pause before that garden-gate,
To breathe the incense of those slumbering roses?
No footstep stirred: the hated world all slept,
Save only thee and me--(O Heaven!--O God!
How my heart beats in coupling those two words!)--
Save only thee and me. I paused--I looked--
And in an instant all things disappeared.
(Ah, bear in mind this garden was enchanted!)
The pearly lustre of the moon went out:
The mossy banks and the meandering paths,
The happy flowers and the repining trees,
Were seen no more: the very roses' odors
Died in the arms of the adoring airs.
All--all expired save thee--save less than thou:
Save only the divine light in thine eyes--
Save but the soul in thine uplifted eyes.
I saw but them--they were the world to me.
I saw but them--saw only them for hours--

Saw only them until the moon went down.
What wild heart-histories seemed to lie unwritten
Upon those crystalline, celestial spheres!
How dark a woe! yet how sublime a hope!
How silently serene a sea of pride!
How daring an ambition! yet how deep--
How fathomless a capacity for love!

But now, at length, dear Dian sank from sight,
Into a western couch of thunder-cloud;
And thou, a ghost, amid the entombing trees
Didst glide away. Only thine eyes remained.
They would not go--they never yet have gone.
Lighting my lonely pathway home that night,
They have not left me (as my hopes have) since.
They follow me--they lead me through the years.

They are my ministers--yet I their slave.
Their office is to illumine and enkindle--
My duty, to be saved by their bright light,
And purified in their electric fire,
And sanctified in their elysian fire.
They fill my soul with Beauty (which is Hope),
And are far up in Heaven--the stars I kneel to
In the sad, silent watches of my night;
While even in the meridian glare of day
I see them still--two sweetly scintillant
Venuses, unextinguished by the sun!

1846.

ANNABEL LEE

It was many and many a year ago,
    In a kingdom by the sea,
That a maiden there lived whom you may know
    By the name of ANNABEL LEE;
And this maiden she lived with no other thought
    Than to love and be loved by me.

I was a child and she was a child,
    In this kingdom by the sea:
But we loved with a love that was more than love--
    I and my ANNABEL LEE;
With a love that the winged seraphs of heaven
    Coveted her and me.

And this was the reason that, long ago,
    In this kingdom by the sea,
A wind blew out of a cloud, chilling
    My beautiful ANNABEL LEE;
So that her highborn kinsmen came
    And bore her away from me,
To shut her up in a sepulchre
    In this kingdom by the sea.

The angels, not half so happy in heaven,
    Went envying her and me--
Yes!--that was the reason (as all men know,
    In this kingdom by the sea)
That the wind came out of the cloud by night,
    Chilling and killing my ANNABEL LEE.

But our love it was stronger by far than the love
    Of those who were older than we--
    Of many far wiser than we--
And neither the angels in heaven above,
    Nor the demons down under the sea,
Can ever dissever my soul from the soul
    Of the beautiful ANNABEL LEE.

For the moon never beams without bringing me dreams
    Of the beautiful ANNABEL LEE;
And the stars never rise but I see the bright eyes
    Of the beautiful ANNABEL LEE;

And so, all the night-tide, I lie down by the side
Of my darling, my darling, my life and my bride,
   In her sepulchre there by the sea--
   In her tomb by the side of the sea.

A VALENTINE

For her this rhyme is penned, whose luminous eyes,
    Brightly expressive as the twins of Leda,
Shall find her own sweet name, that, nestling lies
    Upon the page, enwrapped from every reader.
Search narrowly the lines!--they hold a treasure
    Divine--a talisman--an amulet
That must be worn at heart. Search well the measure--
    The words--the syllables! Do not forget
The trivialest point, or you may lose your labor!
    And yet there is in this no Gordian knot
Which one might not undo without a sabre,
    If one could merely comprehend the plot.
Enwritten upon the leaf where now are peering
    Eyes scintillating soul, there lie perdus
Three eloquent words oft uttered in the hearing
    Of poets by poets--as the name is a poet's, too.
Its letters, although naturally lying
    Like the knight Pinto--Mendez Ferdinando--
Still form a synonym for Truth--Cease trying!
    You will not read the riddle, though you do the best you can do.

1846.

[To discover the names in this and the following poem, read the first letter of the first line in connection with the second letter of the second line, the third letter of the third line, the fourth, of the fourth and so on, to the end.]

AN ENIGMA

"Seldom we find," says Solomon Don Dunce,
    "Half an idea in the profoundest sonnet.
    Through all the flimsy things we see at once
    As easily as through a Naples bonnet--
    Trash of all trash!--how can a lady don it?
    Yet heavier far than your Petrarchan stuff--
    Owl-downy nonsense that the faintest puff
    Twirls into trunk-paper the while you con it."
    And, veritably, Sol is right enough.
    The general tuckermanities are arrant
    Bubbles--ephemeral and so transparent--
    But this is, now--you may depend upon it--
    Stable, opaque, immortal--all by dint
    Of the dear names that lie concealed within't.

[See note after previous poem.]

1847.

TO MY MOTHER

Because I feel that, in the Heavens above,
    The angels, whispering to one another,
Can find, among their burning terms of love,
    None so devotional as that of "Mother,"
Therefore by that dear name I long have called you--
    You who are more than mother unto me,
And fill my heart of hearts, where Death installed you,
    In setting my Virginia's spirit free.
My mother--my own mother, who died early,
    Was but the mother of myself; but you
Are mother to the one I loved so dearly,
    And thus are dearer than the mother I knew
By that infinity with which my wife
    Was dearer to my soul than its soul-life.

1849.

[The above was addressed to the poet's mother-in-law, Mrs. Clemm.--Ed.]

FOR ANNIE

Thank Heaven! the crisis--
    The danger is past,
And the lingering illness
    Is over at last--
And the fever called "Living"
    Is conquered at last.

Sadly, I know,
    I am shorn of my strength,
And no muscle I move
    As I lie at full length--
But no matter!--I feel
    I am better at length.

And I rest so composedly,
    Now in my bed,
That any beholder
    Might fancy me dead--
Might start at beholding me
    Thinking me dead.

The moaning and groaning,
    The sighing and sobbing,
Are quieted now,
    With that horrible throbbing
At heart:--ah, that horrible,
    Horrible throbbing!

The sickness--the nausea--
    The pitiless pain--
Have ceased, with the fever
    That maddened my brain--
With the fever called "Living"
    That burned in my brain.

And oh! of all tortures
    That torture the worst
Has abated--the terrible
    Torture of thirst,
For the naphthaline river
    Of Passion accurst:--
I have drank of a water

That quenches all thirst:--

Of a water that flows,
    With a lullaby sound,
From a spring but a very few
    Feet under ground--
From a cavern not very far
    Down under ground.

And ah! let it never
    Be foolishly said
That my room it is gloomy
    And narrow my bed--
For man never slept
    In a different bed;
And, to sleep, you must slumber
    In just such a bed.

My tantalized spirit
    Here blandly reposes,
Forgetting, or never
    Regretting its roses--
Its old agitations
    Of myrtles and roses:

For now, while so quietly
    Lying, it fancies
A holier odor
    About it, of pansies--
A rosemary odor,
    Commingled with pansies--
With rue and the beautiful
    Puritan pansies.

And so it lies happily,
    Bathing in many
A dream of the truth
    And the beauty of Annie--
Drowned in a bath
    Of the tresses of Annie.

She tenderly kissed me,
    She fondly caressed,
And then I fell gently
    To sleep on her breast--
Deeply to sleep
    From the heaven of her breast.

When the light was extinguished,
    She covered me warm,
And she prayed to the angels
    To keep me from harm--
To the queen of the angels
    To shield me from harm.

And I lie so composedly,
    Now in my bed
(Knowing her love)
    That you fancy me dead--
And I rest so contentedly,
    Now in my bed,
(With her love at my breast)
    That you fancy me dead--
That you shudder to look at me.
    Thinking me dead.

But my heart it is brighter
    Than all of the many
Stars in the sky,
    For it sparkles with Annie--
It glows with the light
    Of the love of my Annie--
With the thought of the light
    Of the eyes of my Annie.

1849.

TO F—

Beloved! amid the earnest woes
    That crowd around my earthly path--
(Drear path, alas! where grows
Not even one lonely rose)--
    My soul at least a solace hath
In dreams of thee, and therein knows
An Eden of bland repose.

And thus thy memory is to me
    Like some enchanted far-off isle
In some tumultuous sea--
Some ocean throbbing far and free
    With storm--but where meanwhile
Serenest skies continually
    Just o'er that one bright inland smile.

1845.

TO FRANCES S. OSGOOD.

Thou wouldst be loved?--then let thy heart
    From its present pathway part not;
Being everything which now thou art,
    Be nothing which thou art not.
So with the world thy gentle ways,
    Thy grace, thy more than beauty,
Shall be an endless theme of praise.
    And love a simple duty.

1845.

ELDORADO

    Gaily bedight,
    A gallant knight,
In sunshine and in shadow,
    Had journeyed long,
    Singing a song,
In search of Eldorado.
    But he grew old--
    This knight so bold--
And o'er his heart a shadow
    Fell as he found
    No spot of ground
That looked like Eldorado.

And, as his strength
    Failed him at length,
He met a pilgrim shadow--
    "Shadow," said he,
    "Where can it be--
This land of Eldorado?"

"Over the Mountains
    Of the Moon,
Down the Valley of the Shadow,
    Ride, boldly ride,"
    The shade replied,
"If you seek for Eldorado!"

    1849.

EULALIE

    I dwelt alone
    In a world of moan,
   And my soul was a stagnant tide,
Till the fair and gentle Eulalie became my blushing bride--
Till the yellow-haired young Eulalie became my smiling bride.
    Ah, less--less bright
    The stars of the night
   Than the eyes of the radiant girl!
    And never a flake
    That the vapor can make
   With the moon-tints of purple and pearl,
Can vie with the modest Eulalie's most unregarded curl--
Can compare with the bright-eyed Eulalie's most humble and careless curl.
    Now Doubt--now Pain
    Come never again,
   For her soul gives me sigh for sigh,
    And all day long
    Shines, bright and strong,
   Astarté within the sky,
While ever to her dear Eulalie upturns her matron eye--
While ever to her young Eulalie upturns her violet eye.

1845.

A DREAM WITHIN A DREAM

Take this kiss upon the brow!
And, in parting from you now,
Thus much let me avow--
You are not wrong, who deem
That my days have been a dream:
Yet if hope has flown away
In a night, or in a day,
In a vision or in none,
Is it therefore the less gone?
All that we see or seem
Is but a dream within a dream.

I stand amid the roar
Of a surf-tormented shore,
And I hold within my hand
Grains of the golden sand--
How few! yet how they creep
Through my fingers to the deep
While I weep--while I weep!
O God! can I not grasp
Them with a tighter clasp?
O God! can I not save
One from the pitiless wave?
Is all that we see or seem
But a dream within a dream?

    1849.

TO MARIE LOUISE (SHEW)

Of all who hail thy presence as the morning--
Of all to whom thine absence is the night--
The blotting utterly from out high heaven
The sacred sun--of all who, weeping, bless thee
Hourly for hope--for life--ah, above all,
For the resurrection of deep buried faith
In truth, in virtue, in humanity--
Of all who, on despair's unhallowed bed
Lying down to die, have suddenly arisen
At thy soft-murmured words, "Let there be light!"
At thy soft-murmured words that were fulfilled
In thy seraphic glancing of thine eyes--
Of all who owe thee most, whose gratitude
Nearest resembles worship,--oh, remember
The truest, the most fervently devoted,
And think that these weak lines are written by him--
By him who, as he pens them, thrills to think
His spirit is communing with an angel's.

   1847.

TO MARIE LOUISE (SHEW)

Not long ago, the writer of these lines,
In the mad pride of intellectuality,
Maintained "the power of words"--denied that ever
A thought arose within the human brain
Beyond the utterance of the human tongue:
And now, as if in mockery of that boast,
Two words--two foreign soft dissyllables--
Italian tones, made only to be murmured
By angels dreaming in the moonlit "dew
That hangs like chains of pearl on Hermon hill,"--
Have stirred from out the abysses of his heart,
Unthought-like thoughts that are the souls of thought,
Richer, far wilder, far diviner visions
Than even the seraph harper, Israfel,
(Who has "the sweetest voice of all God's creatures,")
Could hope to utter. And I! my spells are broken.
The pen falls powerless from my shivering hand.
With thy dear name as text, though hidden by thee,
I cannot write--I cannot speak or think--
Alas, I cannot feel; for 'tis not feeling,
This standing motionless upon the golden
Threshold of the wide-open gate of dreams,
Gazing, entranced, adown the gorgeous vista,
And thrilling as I see, upon the right,
Upon the left, and all the way along,
Amid empurpled vapors, far away
To where the prospect terminates--thee only!

THE CITY IN THE SEA

Lo! Death has reared himself a throne
In a strange city lying alone
Far down within the dim West,
Where the good and the bad and the worst and the best
Have gone to their eternal rest.
There shrines and palaces and towers
(Time-eaten towers and tremble not!)
Resemble nothing that is ours.
Around, by lifting winds forgot,
Resignedly beneath the sky
The melancholy waters lie.

No rays from the holy Heaven come down
On the long night-time of that town;
But light from out the lurid sea
Streams up the turrets silently--
Gleams up the pinnacles far and free--
Up domes--up spires--up kingly halls--
Up fanes--up Babylon-like walls--
Up shadowy long-forgotten bowers
Of sculptured ivy and stone flowers--
Up many and many a marvellous shrine
Whose wreathed friezes intertwine
The viol, the violet, and the vine.

Resignedly beneath the sky
The melancholy waters lie.
So blend the turrets and shadows there
That all seem pendulous in air,
While from a proud tower in the town
Death looks gigantically down.

There open fanes and gaping graves
Yawn level with the luminous waves;
But not the riches there that lie
In each idol's diamond eye--
Not the gaily-jewelled dead
Tempt the waters from their bed;
For no ripples curl, alas!
Along that wilderness of glass--
No swellings tell that winds may be
Upon some far-off happier sea--

Edgar Allan Poe

No heavings hint that winds have been
On seas less hideously serene.

But lo, a stir is in the air!
The wave--there is a movement there!
As if the towers had thrust aside,
In slightly sinking, the dull tide--
As if their tops had feebly given
A void within the filmy Heaven.
The waves have now a redder glow--
The hours are breathing faint and low--
And when, amid no earthly moans,
Down, down that town shall settle hence,
Hell, rising from a thousand thrones,
Shall do it reverence.

    1835?

THE SLEEPER

At midnight, in the month of June,
I stand beneath the mystic moon.
An opiate vapor, dewy, dim,
Exhales from out her golden rim,
And, softly dripping, drop by drop,
Upon the quiet mountain top,
Steals drowsily and musically
Into the universal valley.
The rosemary nods upon the grave;
The lily lolls upon the wave;
Wrapping the fog about its breast,
The ruin moulders into rest;
Looking like Lethe, see! the lake
A conscious slumber seems to take,
And would not, for the world, awake.
All Beauty sleeps!--and lo! where lies
(Her casement open to the skies)
Irene, with her Destinies!

Oh, lady bright! can it be right--
This window open to the night!
The wanton airs, from the tree-top,
Laughingly through the lattice-drop--
The bodiless airs, a wizard rout,
Flit through thy chamber in and out,
And wave the curtain canopy
So fitfully--so fearfully--
Above the closed and fringed lid
'Neath which thy slumb'ring soul lies hid,
That, o'er the floor and down the wall,
Like ghosts the shadows rise and fall!
Oh, lady dear, hast thou no fear?
Why and what art thou dreaming here?
Sure thou art come o'er far-off seas,
A wonder to these garden trees!
Strange is thy pallor! strange thy dress!
Strange, above all, thy length of tress,
And this all-solemn silentness!

The lady sleeps! Oh, may her sleep
Which is enduring, so be deep!
Heaven have her in its sacred keep!

This chamber changed for one more holy,
This bed for one more melancholy,
I pray to God that she may lie
For ever with unopened eye,
While the dim sheeted ghosts go by!

My love, she sleeps! Oh, may her sleep,
As it is lasting, so be deep;
Soft may the worms about her creep!
Far in the forest, dim and old,
For her may some tall vault unfold--
Some vault that oft hath flung its black
And winged panels fluttering back,
Triumphant, o'er the crested palls,
Of her grand family funerals--
Some sepulchre, remote, alone,
Against whose portal she hath thrown,
In childhood many an idle stone--
Some tomb from out whose sounding door
She ne'er shall force an echo more,
Thrilling to think, poor child of sin!
It was the dead who groaned within.

   1845.

BRIDAL BALLAD

The ring is on my hand,
    And the wreath is on my brow;
Satins and jewels grand
Are all at my command.
    And I am happy now.

And my lord he loves me well;
    But, when first he breathed his vow,
I felt my bosom swell--
For the words rang as a knell,
And the voice seemed his who fell
In the battle down the dell,
    And who is happy now.

But he spoke to reassure me,
    And he kissed my pallid brow,
While a reverie came o'er me,
And to the churchyard bore me,
And I sighed to him before me,
Thinking him dead D'Elormie,
    "Oh, I am happy now!"

And thus the words were spoken,
    And thus the plighted vow,
And, though my faith be broken,
And, though my heart be broken,
Behold the golden keys
    That proves me happy now!

Would to God I could awaken
    For I dream I know not how,
And my soul is sorely shaken
Lest an evil step be taken,--
Lest the dead who is forsaken
    May not be happy now.

    1845.

NOTES

1. THE RAVEN

"The Raven" was first published on the 29th January, 1845, in the New York 'Evening Mirror'--a paper its author was then assistant editor of. It was prefaced by the following words, understood to have been written by N. P. Willis:

"We are permitted to copy (in advance of publication) from the second number of the 'American Review', the following remarkable poem by Edgar Poe. In our opinion, it is the most effective single example of 'fugitive poetry' ever published in this country, and unsurpassed in English poetry for subtle conception, masterly ingenuity of versification, and consistent sustaining of imaginative lift and 'pokerishness.' It is one of those 'dainties bred in a book' which we feed on. It will stick to the memory of everybody who reads it."

In the February number of the 'American Review' the poem was published as by "Quarles," and it was introduced by the following note, evidently suggested if not written by Poe himself.

["The following lines from a correspondent--besides the deep, quaint strain of the sentiment, and the curious introduction of some ludicrous touches amidst the serious and impressive, as was doubtless intended by the author--appears to us one of the most felicitous specimens of unique rhyming which has for some time met our eye. The resources of English rhythm for varieties of melody, measure, and sound, producing corresponding diversities of effect, have been thoroughly studied, much more perceived, by very few poets in the language. While the classic tongues, especially the Greek, possess, by power of accent, several advantages for versification over our own, chiefly through greater abundance of spondaic feet, we have other and very great advantages of sound by the modern usage of rhyme. Alliteration is nearly the only effect of that kind which the ancients had in common with us. It will be seen that much of the melody of 'The Raven' arises from alliteration and the studious use of similar sounds in unusual places. In regard to its measure, it may be noted that if all the verses were like the second, they might properly be placed merely in short lines, producing a not uncommon form: but the presence in all the others of one line--mostly the second in the verse" (stanza?)--"which flows continuously, with only an aspirate pause in the middle, like that before the short line in the Sapphio Adonic, while the fifth has at the middle pause no similarity of sound with any part beside, gives the versification an entirely different effect. We could wish the capacities of our noble language in prosody were better understood."

ED. 'Am. Rev.']

2. THE BELLS

The bibliographical history of "The Bells" is curious. The subject, and some lines of the original version, having been suggested by the poet's friend, Mrs. Shew, Poe, when he wrote out the first draft of the poem, headed it, "The Bells. By Mrs. M. A. Shew." This draft, now the editor's property, consists of only seventeen lines, and reads thus:

I.

    The bells!--ah the bells!
    The little silver bells!
How fairy-like a melody there floats
        From their throats--
        From their merry little throats--
        From the silver, tinkling throats
    Of the bells, bells, bells--
        Of the bells!

II.

    The bells!--ah, the bells!
    The heavy iron bells!
How horrible a monody there floats
        From their throats--
        From their deep-toned throats--
        From their melancholy throats
        How I shudder at the notes
    Of the bells, bells, bells--
        Of the bells!

In the autumn of 1848 Poe added another line to this poem, and sent it to the editor of the 'Union Magazine'. It was not published. So, in the following February, the poet forwarded to the same periodical a much enlarged and altered transcript. Three months having elapsed without publication, another revision of the poem, similar to the current version, was sent, and in the following October was published in the 'Union Magazine'.

3. ULALUME

This poem was first published in Colton's 'American Review' for December 1847, as "To----Ulalume: a Ballad." Being reprinted immediately in the 'Home Journal', it was copied into various publications with the name of the editor, N. P. Willis, appended, and was ascribed to him. When first published, it contained the following additional stanza which Poe subsequently, at the suggestion of Mrs. Whitman wisely suppressed:

Said we then--the two, then--"Ah, can it
    Have been that the woodlandish ghouls--
    The pitiful, the merciful ghouls--

To bar up our path and to ban it
    From the secret that lies in these wolds--
Had drawn up the spectre of a planet
    From the limbo of lunary souls--
This sinfully scintillant planet
    From the Hell of the planetary souls?"

4. TO HELEN

"To Helen" (Mrs. S. Helen Whitman) was not published Until November 1848, although written several months earlier. It first appeared in the 'Union Magazine' and with the omission, contrary to the knowledge or desire of Poe, of the line, "Oh, God! oh, Heaven--how my heart beats in coupling those two words".

5. ANNABEL LEE

"Annabel Lee" was written early in 1849, and is evidently an expression of the poet's undying love for his deceased bride although at least one of his lady admirers deemed it a response to her admiration. Poe sent a copy of the ballad to the 'Union Magazine', in which publication it appeared in January 1850, three months after the author's death. Whilst suffering from "hope deferred" as to its fate, Poe presented a copy of "Annabel Lee" to the editor of the 'Southern Literary Messenger', who published it in the November number of his periodical, a month after Poe's death. In the meantime the poet's own copy, left among his papers, passed into the hands of the person engaged to edit his works, and he quoted the poem in an obituary of Poe in the New York 'Tribune', before any one else had an opportunity of publishing it.

6. A VALENTINE

"A Valentine," one of three poems addressed to Mrs. Osgood, appears to have been written early in 1846.

7. AN ENIGMA

"An Enigma," addressed to Mrs. Sarah Anna Lewig ("Stella"), was sent to that lady in a letter, in November 1847, and the following March appeared in Sartain's 'Union Magazine'.

8. TO MY MOTHER

The sonnet, "To My Mother" (Maria Clemm), was sent for publication to the short-lived 'Flag of our Union', early in 1849, but does not appear to have been issued until after its author's death, when it appeared in the 'Leaflets of Memory' for 1850.

9. FOR ANNIE

"For Annie" was first published in the 'Flag of our Union', in the spring of 1849. Poe, annoyed at some misprints in this issue, shortly afterwards caused a corrected copy to be inserted in the 'Home Journal'.

10. TO F----

"To F----" (Frances Sargeant Osgood) appeared in the 'Broadway Journal' for April 1845. These lines are but slightly varied from those inscribed "To Mary," in the 'Southern Literary Messenger' for July 1835, and subsequently republished, with the two stanzas transposed, in 'Graham's Magazine' for March 1842, as "To One Departed."

11. TO FRANCES S. OSGOOD

"To F--s S. O--d," a portion of the poet's triune tribute to Mrs. Osgood, was published in the 'Broadway Journal' for September 1845. The earliest version of these lines appeared in the 'Southern Literary Messenger' for September 1835, as "Lines written in an Album," and was addressed to Eliza White, the proprietor's daughter. Slightly revised, the poem reappeared in Burton's 'Gentleman's Magazine' for August, 1839, as "To----."

12. ELDORADO

Although "Eldorado" was published during Poe's lifetime, in 1849, in the 'Flag of our Union', it does not appear to have ever received the author's finishing touches.

13. EULALIE

"Eulalie--a Song" first appears in Colton's 'American Review' for July, 1845.

14. A DREAM WITHIN A DREAM

"A Dream within a Dream" does not appear to have been published as a separate poem during its author's lifetime. A portion of it was contained, in 1829, in the piece beginning, "Should my early life seem," and in 1831 some few lines of it were used as a conclusion to "Tamerlane." In 1849 the poet sent a friend all but the first nine lines of the piece as a separate poem, headed "For Annie."

15 TO MARIE LOUISE (SHEW)

"To M----L----S----," addressed to Mrs. Marie Louise Shew, was written in February 1847, and published shortly afterwards. In the first posthumous collection of Poe's poems these lines were, for some reason, included in the "Poems written in Youth," and amongst those poems they have hitherto been included.

16.(2) TO MARIE LOUISE (SHEW)

"To----," a second piece addressed to Mrs. Shew, and written in 1848, was also first published, but in a somewhat faulty form, in the above named posthumous collection.

17. THE CITY IN THE SEA

Under the title of "The Doomed City" the initial version of "The City in the Sea" appeared in the 1831 volume of Poems by Poe: it reappeared as "The City of Sin," in the 'Southern Literary Messenger' for August 1835, whilst the present draft of it first appeared in Colton's 'American Review' for April, 1845.

18. THE SLEEPER

As "Irene," the earliest known version of "The Sleeper," appeared in the 1831 volume. It reappeared in the 'Literary Messenger' for May 1836, and, in its present form, in the 'Broadway Journal' for May 1845.

19. THE BRIDAL BALLAD

"The Bridal Ballad" is first discoverable in the 'Southern Literary Messenger' for January 1837, and, in its present compressed and revised form, was reprinted in the 'Broadway Journal' for August, 1845.

POEMS OF MANHOOD

LENORE

Ah, broken is the golden bowl! the spirit flown forever!
Let the bell toll!--a saintly soul floats on the Stygian river.
And, Guy de Vere, hast thou no tear?--weep now or never more!
See! on yon drear and rigid bier low lies thy love, Lenore!
Come! let the burial rite be read--the funeral song be sung!--
An anthem for the queenliest dead that ever died so young--
A dirge for her, the doubly dead in that she died so young.

"Wretches! ye loved her for her wealth and hated her for her pride,
And when she fell in feeble health, ye blessed her--that she died!
How shall the ritual, then, be read?--the requiem how be sung
By you--by yours, the evil eye,--by yours, the slanderous tongue
That did to death the innocence that died, and died so young?"

Peccavimus; but rave not thus! and let a Sabbath song
Go up to God so solemnly the dead may feel no wrong!
The sweet Lenore hath "gone before," with Hope, that flew beside,
Leaving thee wild for the dear child that should have been thy bride--
For her, the fair and débonnaire, that now so lowly lies,
The life upon her yellow hair but not within her eyes--
The life still there, upon her hair--the death upon her eyes.

"Avaunt! to-night my heart is light. No dirge will I upraise,
But waft the angel on her flight with a pæan of old days!
Let no bell toll!--lest her sweet soul, amid its hallowed mirth,
Should catch the note, as it doth float up from the damned Earth.
To friends above, from fiends below, the indignant ghost is riven--
From Hell unto a high estate far up within the Heaven--
From grief and groan to a golden throne beside the King of Heaven."

    1844.

TO ONE IN PARADISE

Thou wast that all to me, love,
    For which my soul did pine--
A green isle in the sea, love,
    A fountain and a shrine,
All wreathed with fairy fruits and flowers,
And all the flowers were mine.

Ah, dream too bright to last!
    Ah, starry Hope! that didst arise
But to be overcast!
    A voice from out the Future cries,
"On! on!"--but o'er the Past
    (Dim gulf!) my spirit hovering lies
Mute, motionless, aghast!

For, alas! alas! with me
    The light of Life is o'er!
"No more--no more--no more"--
(Such language holds the solemn sea
    To the sands upon the shore)
Shall bloom the thunder-blasted tree,
    Or the stricken eagle soar!

And all my days are trances,
    And all my nightly dreams
Are where thy dark eye glances,
    And where thy footstep gleams--
In what ethereal dances,
    By what eternal streams!

Alas! for that accursed time
    They bore thee o'er the billow,
From love to titled age and crime,
    And an unholy pillow!
From me, and from our misty clime,
    Where weeps the silver willow!

1835

THE COLISEUM

Type of the antique Rome! Rich reliquary
Of lofty contemplation left to Time
By buried centuries of pomp and power!
At length--at length--after so many days
Of weary pilgrimage and burning thirst,
(Thirst for the springs of lore that in thee lie,)
I kneel, an altered and an humble man,
Amid thy shadows, and so drink within
My very soul thy grandeur, gloom, and glory!

Vastness! and Age! and Memories of Eld!
Silence! and Desolation! and dim Night!
I feel ye now--I feel ye in your strength--
O spells more sure than e'er Judæan king
Taught in the gardens of Gethsemane!
O charms more potent than the rapt Chaldee
Ever drew down from out the quiet stars!

Here, where a hero fell, a column falls!
Here, where the mimic eagle glared in gold,
A midnight vigil holds the swarthy bat!
Here, where the dames of Rome their gilded hair
Waved to the wind, now wave the reed and thistle!
Here, where on golden throne the monarch lolled,
Glides, spectre-like, unto his marble home,
Lit by the wan light of the horned moon,
The swift and silent lizard of the stones!

But stay! these walls--these ivy-clad arcades--
These mouldering plinths--these sad and blackened shafts--
These vague entablatures--this crumbling frieze--
These shattered cornices--this wreck--this ruin--
These stones--alas! these gray stones--are they all--
All of the famed, and the colossal left
By the corrosive Hours to Fate and me?

"Not all"--the Echoes answer me--"not all!
Prophetic sounds and loud, arise forever
From us, and from all Ruin, unto the wise,
As melody from Memnon to the Sun.
We rule the hearts of mightiest men--we rule
With a despotic sway all giant minds.

We are not impotent--we pallid stones.
Not all our power is gone--not all our fame--
Not all the magic of our high renown--
Not all the wonder that encircles us--
Not all the mysteries that in us lie--
Not all the memories that hang upon
And cling around about us as a garment,
Clothing us in a robe of more than glory."

   1838.

THE HAUNTED PALACE

In the greenest of our valleys
    By good angels tenanted,
Once a fair and stately palace--
    Radiant palace--reared its head.
In the monarch Thought's dominion--
    It stood there!
Never seraph spread a pinion
    Over fabric half so fair!

Banners yellow, glorious, golden,
    On its roof did float and flow,
(This--all this--was in the olden
    Time long ago),
And every gentle air that dallied,
    In that sweet day,
Along the ramparts plumed and pallid,
    A winged odor went away.

Wanderers in that happy valley,
    Through two luminous windows, saw
Spirits moving musically,
    To a lute's well-tunëd law,
Bound about a throne where, sitting
    (Porphyrogene!)
In state his glory well befitting,
    The ruler of the realm was seen.

And all with pearl and ruby glowing
    Was the fair palace door,
Through which came flowing, flowing, flowing,
    And sparkling evermore,
A troop of Echoes, whose sweet duty
    Was but to sing,
In voices of surpassing beauty,
    The wit and wisdom of their king.

But evil things, in robes of sorrow,
    Assailed the monarch's high estate.
(Ah, let us mourn!--for never morrow
    Shall dawn upon him desolate !)
And round about his home the glory
    That blushed and bloomed,

Is but a dim-remembered story
    Of the old time entombed.

And travellers, now, within that valley,
    Through the red-litten windows see
Vast forms, that move fantastically
    To a discordant melody,
    While, like a ghastly rapid river,
    Through the pale door
A hideous throng rush out forever
    And laugh--but smile no more.

    1838.

THE CONQUEROR WORM

Lo! 'tis a gala night
    Within the lonesome latter years!
An angel throng, bewinged, bedight
    In veils, and drowned in tears,
Sit in a theatre, to see
    A play of hopes and fears,
While the orchestra breathes fitfully
    The music of the spheres.

Mimes, in the form of God on high,
    Mutter and mumble low,
And hither and thither fly--
    Mere puppets they, who come and go
At bidding of vast formless things
    That shift the scenery to and fro,
Flapping from out their Condor wings
    Invisible Wo!

That motley drama--oh, be sure
    It shall not be forgot!
With its Phantom chased for evermore,
    By a crowd that seize it not,
Through a circle that ever returneth in
    To the self-same spot,
And much of Madness, and more of Sin,
    And Horror the soul of the plot.

But see, amid the mimic rout
    A crawling shape intrude!
A blood-red thing that writhes from out
    The scenic solitude!
It writhes!--it writhes!--with mortal pangs
    The mimes become its food,
And the angels sob at vermin fangs
    In human gore imbued.

Out--out are the lights--out all!
    And, over each quivering form,
The curtain, a funeral pall,
    Comes down with the rush of a storm,

Edgar Allan Poe

And the angels, all pallid and wan,
    Uprising, unveiling, affirm
That the play is the tragedy, "Man,"
    And its hero the Conqueror Worm.

1838

SILENCE

There are some qualities--some incorporate things,
    That have a double life, which thus is made
A type of that twin entity which springs
    From matter and light, evinced in solid and shade.
There is a twofold Silence--sea and shore--
    Body and soul. One dwells in lonely places,
    Newly with grass o'ergrown; some solemn graces,
Some human memories and tearful lore,
Render him terrorless: his name's "No More."
He is the corporate Silence: dread him not!
    No power hath he of evil in himself;
But should some urgent fate (untimely lot!)
    Bring thee to meet his shadow (nameless elf,
That haunteth the lone regions where hath trod
No foot of man), commend thyself to God!

1840

DREAMLAND

By a route obscure and lonely,
Haunted by ill angels only,
Where an Eidolon, named NIGHT,
On a black throne reigns upright,
I have reached these lands but newly
From an ultimate dim Thule--
From a wild weird clime that lieth, sublime,
    Out of SPACE--out of TIME.

Bottomless vales and boundless floods,
And chasms, and caves, and Titan woods,
With forms that no man can discover
For the dews that drip all over;
Mountains toppling evermore
Into seas without a shore;
Seas that restlessly aspire,
Surging, unto skies of fire;
Lakes that endlessly outspread
Their lone waters--lone and dead,
Their still waters--still and chilly
With the snows of the lolling lily.

By the lakes that thus outspread
Their lone waters, lone and dead,--
Their sad waters, sad and chilly
With the snows of the lolling lily,--

By the mountains--near the river
Murmuring lowly, murmuring ever,--
By the gray woods,--by the swamp
Where the toad and the newt encamp,--
By the dismal tarns and pools
    Where dwell the Ghouls,--
By each spot the most unholy--
In each nook most melancholy,--

There the traveller meets aghast
Sheeted Memories of the past--
Shrouded forms that start and sigh
As they pass the wanderer by--
White-robed forms of friends long given,
In agony, to the Earth--and Heaven.

For the heart whose woes are legion
'Tis a peaceful, soothing region--
For the spirit that walks in shadow
'Tis--oh, 'tis an Eldorado!
But the traveller, travelling through it,
May not--dare not openly view it;
Never its mysteries are exposed
To the weak human eye unclosed;
So wills its King, who hath forbid
The uplifting of the fringed lid;
And thus the sad Soul that here passes
Beholds it but through darkened glasses.

By a route obscure and lonely,
Haunted by ill angels only.

Where an Eidolon, named NIGHT,
On a black throne reigns upright,
I have wandered home but newly
From this ultimate dim Thule.

    1844

TO ZANTE

Fair isle, that from the fairest of all flowers,
    Thy gentlest of all gentle names dost take!
How many memories of what radiant hours
    At sight of thee and thine at once awake!
How many scenes of what departed bliss!
    How many thoughts of what entombed hopes!
How many visions of a maiden that is
    No more--no more upon thy verdant slopes!

No more! alas, that magical sad sound
    Transforming all! Thy charms shall please no more--
Thy memory no more! Accursed ground
    Henceforward I hold thy flower-enamelled shore,
O hyacinthine isle! O purple Zante!
    "Isola d'oro! Fior di Levante!"

1887.

HYMN

At morn--at noon--at twilight dim--
Maria! thou hast heard my hymn!
In joy and wo--in good and ill--
Mother of God, be with me still!
When the Hours flew brightly by,
And not a cloud obscured the sky,
My soul, lest it should truant be,
Thy grace did guide to thine and thee
Now, when storms of Fate o'ercast
Darkly my Present and my Past,
Let my future radiant shine
With sweet hopes of thee and thine!

    1885.

NOTES

20. LENORE

"Lenore" was published, very nearly in its existing shape, in 'The Pioneer' for 1843, but under the title of "The Pæan"--now first published in the POEMS OF YOUTH--the germ of it appeared in 1831.

21. TO ONE IN PARADISE

"To One in Paradise" was included originally in "The Visionary" (a tale now known as "The Assignation"), in July, 1835, and appeared as a separate poem entitled "To Ianthe in Heaven," in Burton's 'Gentleman's Magazine' for July, 1839. The fifth stanza is now added, for the first time, to the piece.

22. THE COLISEUM

"The Coliseum" appeared in the Baltimore 'Saturday Visitor' ('sic') in 1833, and was republished in the 'Southern Literary Messenger' for August 1835, as "A Prize Poem."

23. THE HAUNTED PALACE

"The Haunted Palace" originally issued in the Baltimore 'American Museum' for April, 1888, was subsequently embodied in that much admired tale, "The Fall of the House of Usher," and published in it in Burton's 'Gentleman's Magazine' for September, 1839. It reappeared in that as a separate poem in the 1845 edition of Poe's poems.

24. THE CONQUEROR WORM

"The Conqueror Worm," then contained in Poe's favorite tale of "Ligeia," was first published in the 'American Museum' for September, 1838. As a separate poem, it reappeared in 'Graham's Magazine' for January, 1843.

25. SILENCE

The sonnet, "Silence," was originally published in Burton's 'Gentleman's Magazine' for April, 1840.

26. DREAMLAND

The first known publication of "Dreamland" was in 'Graham's Magazine' for June, 1844.

37. TO ZANTE

The "Sonnet to Zante" is not discoverable earlier than January, 1837, when it appeared in the 'Southern Literary Messenger'.

28. HYMN

The initial version of the "Catholic Hymn" was contained in the story of "Morella," and published in the 'Southern Literary Messenger' for April, 1885. The lines as they now stand, and with their present title, were first published in the 'Broadway Journal for August', 1845.

SCENES FROM "POLITIAN"
AN UNPUBLISHED DRAMA

I.

ROME.--A Hall in a Palace. ALESSANDRA and CASTIGLIONE

Alessandra.   Thou art sad, Castiglione.

Castiglione. Sad!--not I.
     Oh, I'm the happiest, happiest man in Rome!
     A few days more, thou knowest, my Alessandra,
     Will make thee mine. Oh, I am very happy!

Aless.   Methinks thou hast a singular way of showing
     Thy happiness--what ails thee, cousin of mine?
     Why didst thou sigh so deeply?

Cas. Did I sigh?
     I was not conscious of it. It is a fashion,
     A silly--a most silly fashion I have
     When I am very happy. Did I sigh? (sighing.)

Aless.   Thou didst. Thou art not well. Thou hast indulged
     Too much of late, and I am vexed to see it.
     Late hours and wine, Castiglione,--these
     Will ruin thee! thou art already altered--
     Thy looks are haggard--nothing so wears away
     The constitution as late hours and wine.

Cas. *(musing)*. Nothing, fair cousin, nothing--
     Not even deep sorrow--
     Wears it away like evil hours and wine.
     I will amend.

Aless.   Do it! I would have thee drop
     Thy riotous company, too--fellows low born
     Ill suit the like of old Di Broglio's heir
     And Alessandra's husband.

Cas. I will drop them.

Aless.   Thou wilt--thou must. Attend thou also more
              To thy dress and equipage--they are over plain
              For thy lofty rank and fashion--much depends
              Upon appearances.

Cas.   I'll see to it.

Aless.   Then see to it!--pay more attention, sir,
              To a becoming carriage--much thou wantest
              In dignity.

Cas.   Much, much, oh, much I want
              In proper dignity.

Aless.
(haughtily).   Thou mockest me, sir!

Cos.
(abstractedly). Sweet, gentle Lalage!

Aless.   Heard I aright?
              I speak to him--he speaks of Lalage?
              Sir Count!
        (places her hand on his shoulder)
                        what art thou dreaming?
              He's not well!
              What ails thee, sir?

Cas.*(starting).* Cousin! fair cousin!--madam!
              I crave thy pardon--indeed I am not well--
              Your hand from off my shoulder, if you please.
              This air is most oppressive!--Madam--the Duke!

Enter Di Broglio.

Di Broglio.   My son, I've news for thee!--hey!
              --what's the matter?

        (observing Alessandra).

              I' the pouts? Kiss her, Castiglione! kiss her,
              You dog! and make it up, I say, this minute!
              I've news for you both. Politian is expected
              Hourly in Rome--Politian, Earl of Leicester!
              We'll have him at the wedding. 'Tis his first visit
              To the imperial city.

Aless.   What! Politian
              Of Britain, Earl of Leicester?

Di Brog. The same, my love.
             We'll have him at the wedding. A man quite young
             In years, but gray in fame. I have not seen him,
             But Rumor speaks of him as of a prodigy
             Pre-eminent in arts, and arms, and wealth,
             And high descent. We'll have him at the wedding.

Aless.   I have heard much of this Politian.
             Gay, volatile and giddy--is he not,
             And little given to thinking?

Di Brog. Far from it, love.
             No branch, they say, of all philosophy
             So deep abstruse he has not mastered it.
             Learned as few are learned.

Aless.   'Tis very strange!
             I have known men have seen Politian
             And sought his company. They speak of him
             As of one who entered madly into life,
             Drinking the cup of pleasure to the dregs.

Cas.   Ridiculous! Now I have seen Politian
             And know him well--nor learned nor mirthful he.
             He is a dreamer, and shut out
             From common passions.

Di Brog. Children, we disagree.
             Let us go forth and taste the fragrant air
             Of the garden. Did I dream, or did I hear
             Politian was a melancholy man?

         (Exeunt.)

II.

ROME.--A Lady's Apartment, with a window open and looking into a garden. LALAGE, in deep mourning, reading at a table on which lie some books and a hand-mirror. In the background JACINTA (a servant maid) leans carelessly upon a chair.

Lalage.   Jacinta! is it thou?

Jacinta
(pertly). Yes, ma'am, I'm here.

Lal.   I did not know, Jacinta, you were in waiting.
             Sit down!--let not my presence trouble you--
             Sit down!--for I am humble, most humble.

Jac. *(aside)*. 'Tis time.

(Jacinta seats herself in a side-long manner upon the chair, resting her elbows upon the back, and regarding her mistress with a contemptuous look. Lalage continues to read.)

Lal.   "It in another climate, so he said,
            Bore a bright golden flower, but not i' this soil!"

        (pauses--turns over some leaves and resumes.)

            "No lingering winters there, nor snow, nor shower--
            But Ocean ever to refresh mankind
            Breathes the shrill spirit of the western wind"
            Oh, beautiful!--most beautiful!--how like
            To what my fevered soul doth dream of Heaven!
            O happy land! (pauses) She died!--the maiden died!
            O still more happy maiden who couldst die!
            Jacinta!

(Jacinta returns no answer, and Lalage presently resumes.)

            Again!--a similar tale
            Told of a beauteous dame beyond the sea!
            Thus speaketh one Ferdinand in the words of the play--
            "She died full young"--one Bossola answers him--
            "I think not so--her infelicity
            Seemed to have years too many"--Ah, luckless lady!
            Jacinta! *(still no answer.)*
            Here's a far sterner story--
            But like--oh, very like in its despair--
            Of that Egyptian queen, winning so easily
            A thousand hearts--losing at length her own.
            She died. Thus endeth the history--and her maids
            Lean over her and keep--two gentle maids
            With gentle names--Eiros and Charmion!
            Rainbow and Dove!--Jacinta!

Jac.
(pettishly).   Madam, what is it?

Lal.   Wilt thou, my good Jacinta, be so kind
           As go down in the library and bring me
           The Holy Evangelists?

Jac.   Pshaw!

       (Exit)

Lal.   If there be balm
>For the wounded spirit in Gilead, it is there!
>Dew in the night time of my bitter trouble
>Will there be found--"dew sweeter far than that
>Which hangs like chains of pearl on Hermon hill."

(re-enter Jacinta, and throws a volume on the table.)

>There, ma'am, 's the book.
(aside.) Indeed she is very troublesome.

Lal.
(astonished). What didst thou say, Jacinta?
>Have I done aught
>To grieve thee or to vex thee?--I am sorry.
>For thou hast served me long and ever been
>Trustworthy and respectful.

>*(resumes her reading.)*

Jac. *(aside.)* I can't believe
>She has any more jewels--no--no--she gave me all.

Lal.   What didst thou say, Jacinta? Now I bethink me
>Thou hast not spoken lately of thy wedding.
>How fares good Ugo?--and when is it to be?
>Can I do aught?--is there no further aid
>Thou needest, Jacinta?

Jac. *(aside.)* Is there no further aid!
>That's meant for me. I'm sure, madam, you need not
>Be always throwing those jewels in my teeth.

Lal.   Jewels! Jacinta,--now indeed, Jacinta,
>I thought not of the jewels.

Jac.   Oh, perhaps not!
>But then I might have sworn it. After all,
>There's Ugo says the ring is only paste,
>For he's sure the Count Castiglione never
>Would have given a real diamond to such as you;
>And at the best I'm certain, madam, you cannot
>Have use for jewels now. But I might have sworn it.

>*(Exit)*

(Lalage bursts into tears and leans her head upon the table--after a short pause raises it.)

Lal.   Poor Lalage!--and is it come to this?
            Thy servant maid!--but courage!--'tis but a viper
            Whom thou hast cherished to sting thee to the soul!

         (taking up the mirror)

            Ha! here at least's a friend--too much a friend
            In earlier days--a friend will not deceive thee.
            Fair mirror and true! now tell me (for thou canst)
            A tale--a pretty tale--and heed thou not
            Though it be rife with woe. It answers me.
            It speaks of sunken eyes, and wasted cheeks,
            And beauty long deceased--remembers me,
            Of Joy departed--Hope, the Seraph Hope,
            Inurned and entombed!--now, in a tone
            Low, sad, and solemn, but most audible,
            Whispers of early grave untimely yawning
            For ruined maid. Fair mirror and true!--thou liest not!
            Thou hast no end to gain--no heart to break--
            Castiglione lied who said he loved----
            Thou true--he false!--false!--false!

(While she speaks, a monk enters her apartment and approaches unobserved)

Monk.   Refuge thou hast,
            Sweet daughter! in Heaven. Think of eternal things!
            Give up thy soul to penitence, and pray!

Lal.
(arising hurriedly). I cannot pray!--My soul is at war with God!
            The frightful sounds of merriment below;
            Disturb my senses--go! I cannot pray--
            The sweet airs from the garden worry me!
            Thy presence grieves me--go!--thy priestly raiment
            Fills me with dread--thy ebony crucifix
            With horror and awe!

Monk.   Think of thy precious soul!

Lal.   Think of my early days!--think of my father
            And mother in Heaven! think of our quiet home,
            And the rivulet that ran before the door!
            Think of my little sisters!--think of them!
            And think of me!--think of my trusting love
            And confidence--his vows--my ruin--think--think
            Of my unspeakable misery!----begone!
            Yet stay! yet stay!--what was it thou saidst of prayer
            And penitence? Didst thou not speak of faith
            And vows before the throne?

Monk.   I did.

Lal.   'Tis well.
>There is a vow 'twere fitting should be made--
>A sacred vow, imperative and urgent,
>A solemn vow!

Monk.   Daughter, this zeal is well!

Lal.   Father, this zeal is anything but well!
>Hast thou a crucifix fit for this thing?
>A crucifix whereon to register
>This sacred vow? (he hands her his own.)
>Not that--Oh! no!--no!--no (shuddering.)
>Not that! Not that!--I tell thee, holy man,
>Thy raiments and thy ebony cross affright me!
>Stand back! I have a crucifix myself,--
>I have a crucifix! Methinks 'twere fitting
>The deed--the vow--the symbol of the deed--
>And the deed's register should tally, father!

(draws a cross-handled dagger and raises it on high.)

>Behold the cross wherewith a vow like mine
>Is written in heaven!

Monk.   Thy words are madness, daughter,
>And speak a purpose unholy--thy lips are livid--
>Thine eyes are wild--tempt not the wrath divine!
>Pause ere too late!--oh, be not--be not rash!
>Swear not the oath--oh, swear it not!

Lal.   'Tis sworn!

III.

An Apartment in a Palace. POLITIAN and BALDAZZAR.

Baldazzar.   Arouse thee now, Politian!
>Thou must not--nay indeed, indeed, thou shalt not
>Give way unto these humors. Be thyself!
>Shake off the idle fancies that beset thee
>And live, for now thou diest!

Politian. Not so, Baldazzar!
>Surely I live.

Bal.   Politian, it doth grieve me
>To see thee thus!

Pol. Baldazzar, it doth grieve me
        To give thee cause for grief, my honored friend.
        Command me, sir! what wouldst thou have me do?
        At thy behest I will shake off that nature
        Which from my forefathers I did inherit,
        Which with my mother's milk I did imbibe,
        And be no more Politian, but some other.
        Command me, sir!

Bal. To the field then--to the field--
        To the senate or the field.

Pol. Alas! alas!
        There is an imp would follow me even there!
        There is an imp hath followed me even there!
        There is--what voice was that?

Bal. I heard it not.
        I heard not any voice except thine own,
        And the echo of thine own.

Pol. Then I but dreamed.

Bal. Give not thy soul to dreams: the camp--the court
        Befit thee--Fame awaits thee--Glory calls--
        And her the trumpet-tongued thou wilt not hear
        In hearkening to imaginary sounds
        And phantom voices.

Pol. It is a phantom voice!
        Didst thou not hear it then?

Bal I heard it not.

Pol. Thou heardst it not!--Baldazzar, speak no more
        To me, Politian, of thy camps and courts.
        Oh! I am sick, sick, sick, even unto death,
        Of the hollow and high-sounding vanities
        Of the populous Earth! Bear with me yet awhile
        We have been boys together--school-fellows--
        And now are friends--yet shall not be so long--
        For in the Eternal City thou shalt do me
        A kind and gentle office, and a Power--
        A Power august, benignant, and supreme--
        Shall then absolve thee of all further duties
        Unto thy friend.

Bal. Thou speakest a fearful riddle
        I will not understand.

Pol.   Yet now as Fate
             Approaches, and the Hours are breathing low,
             The sands of Time are changed to golden grains,
             And dazzle me, Baldazzar. Alas! alas!
             I cannot die, having within my heart
             So keen a relish for the beautiful
             As hath been kindled within it. Methinks the air
             Is balmier now than it was wont to be--
             Rich melodies are floating in the winds--
             A rarer loveliness bedecks the earth--
             And with a holier lustre the quiet moon
             Sitteth in Heaven.--Hist! hist! thou canst not say
             Thou hearest not now, Baldazzar?

Bal.   Indeed I hear not.

Pol.   Not hear it!--listen--now--listen!--the faintest sound
             And yet the sweetest that ear ever heard!
             A lady's voice!--and sorrow in the tone!
             Baldazzar, it oppresses me like a spell!
             Again!--again!--how solemnly it falls
             Into my heart of hearts! that eloquent voice
             Surely I never heard--yet it were well
             Had I but heard it with its thrilling tones
             In earlier days!

Bal.   I myself hear it now.
             Be still!--the voice, if I mistake not greatly,
             Proceeds from younder lattice--which you may see
             Very plainly through the window--it belongs,
             Does it not? unto this palace of the Duke.
             The singer is undoubtedly beneath
             The roof of his Excellency--and perhaps
             Is even that Alessandra of whom he spoke
             As the betrothed of Castiglione,
             His son and heir.

Pol.   Be still!--it comes again!

Voice
(very faintly). "And is thy heart so strong[1]
             As for to leave me thus,
             That have loved thee so long,
             In wealth and woe among?
             And is thy heart so strong
             As for to leave me thus?
             Say nay! say nay!"

Bal.   The song is English, and I oft have heard it
            In merry England--never so plaintively--
            Hist! hist! it comes again!

Voice
(more loudly). "Is it so strong
            As for to leave me thus,
            That have loved thee so long,
            In wealth and woe among?
            And is thy heart so strong
            As for to leave me thus?
            Say nay! say nay!"

Bal.   'Tis hushed and all is still!

Pol.   All is not still.

Bal.   Let us go down.

Pol.   Go down, Baldazzar, go!

Bal.   The hour is growing late--the Duke awaits us,--
            Thy presence is expected in the hall
            Below. What ails thee, Earl Politian?

Voice
(distinctly). "Who have loved thee so long,
            In wealth and woe among,
            And is thy heart so strong?
            Say nay! say nay!"

Bal.   Let us descend!--'tis time. Politian, give
            These fancies to the wind. Remember, pray,
            Your bearing lately savored much of rudeness
            Unto the Duke. Arouse thee! and remember!

Pol.   Remember? I do. Lead on! I do remember.

        (going).

            Let us descend. Believe me I would give,
            Freely would give the broad lands of my earldom
            To look upon the face hidden by yon lattice--
            "To gaze upon that veiled face, and hear
            Once more that silent tongue."

Bal.   Let me beg you, sir,
            Descend with me--the Duke may be offended.
            Let us go down, I pray you.

Voice *(loudly)*. Say nay!--say nay!

Pol. *(aside)*. 'Tis strange!--'tis very strange--methought
      the voice
      Chimed in with my desires and bade me stay!

  (Approaching the window)

      Sweet voice! I heed thee, and will surely stay.
      Now be this fancy, by heaven, or be it Fate,
      Still will I not descend. Baldazzar, make
      Apology unto the Duke for me;
      I go not down to-night.

Bal.   Your lordship's pleasure
      Shall be attended to. Good-night, Politian.

Pol.   Good-night, my friend, good-night.

IV.

The Gardens of a Palace--Moonlight. LALAGE and POLITIAN.

Lalage.   And dost thou speak of love
      To me, Politian?--dost thou speak of love
      To Lalage?--ah woe--ah woe is me!
      This mockery is most cruel--most cruel indeed!

Politian. Weep not! oh, sob not thus!--thy bitter tears
      Will madden me. Oh, mourn not, Lalage--
      Be comforted! I know--I know it all,
      And still I speak of love. Look at me, brightest,
      And beautiful Lalage!--turn here thine eyes!
      Thou askest me if I could speak of love,
      Knowing what I know, and seeing what I have seen
      Thou askest me that--and thus I answer thee--
      Thus on my bended knee I answer thee. *(kneeling.)*
      Sweet Lalage, I love thee--love thee--love thee;
      Thro' good and ill--thro' weal and woe, I love thee.
      Not mother, with her first-born on her knee,
      Thrills with intenser love than I for thee.
      Not on God's altar, in any time or clime,
      Burned there a holier fire than burneth now
      Within my spirit for thee. And do I love?

  (arising.)

      Even for thy woes I love thee--even for thy woes--
      Thy beauty and thy woes.

Lal. Alas, proud Earl,
    Thou dost forget thyself, remembering me!
    How, in thy father's halls, among the maidens
    Pure and reproachless of thy princely line,
    Could the dishonored Lalage abide?
    Thy wife, and with a tainted memory--
    My seared and blighted name, how would it tally
    With the ancestral honors of thy house,
    And with thy glory?

Pol. Speak not to me of glory!
    I hate--I loathe the name; I do abhor
    The unsatisfactory and ideal thing.
    Art thou not Lalage, and I Politian?
    Do I not love--art thou not beautiful--
    What need we more? Ha! glory! now speak not of it:
    By all I hold most sacred and most solemn--
    By all my wishes now--my fears hereafter--
    By all I scorn on earth and hope in heaven--
    There is no deed I would more glory in,
    Than in thy cause to scoff at this same glory
    And trample it under foot. What matters it--
    What matters it, my fairest, and my best,
    That we go down unhonored and forgotten
    Into the dust--so we descend together?
    Descend together--and then--and then perchance--

Lal. Why dost thou pause, Politian?

Pol. And then perchance
    Arise together, Lalage, and roam
    The starry and quiet dwellings of the blest,
    And still--

Lal. Why dost thou pause, Politian?

Pol. And still together--together.

Lal. Now, Earl of Leicester!
    Thou lovest me, and in my heart of hearts
    I feel thou lovest me truly.

Pol. O Lalage!

    (throwing himself upon his knee.)

        And lovest thou me?

Lal.   Hist! hush! within the gloom
             Of yonder trees methought a figure passed--
             A spectral figure, solemn, and slow, and noiseless--
             Like the grim shadow Conscience, solemn and noiseless.

       (walks across and returns.)

             I was mistaken--'twas but a giant bough
             Stirred by the autumn wind. Politian!

Pol.   My Lalage--my love! why art thou moved?
             Why dost thou turn so pale? Not Conscience self,
             Far less a shadow which thou likenest to it,
             Should shake the firm spirit thus. But the night wind
             Is chilly--and these melancholy boughs
             Throw over all things a gloom.

Lal.   Politian!
             Thou speakest to me of love. Knowest thou the land
             With which all tongues are busy--a land new found--
             Miraculously found by one of Genoa--
             A thousand leagues within the golden west?
             A fairy land of flowers, and fruit, and sunshine,--
             And crystal lakes, and over-arching forests,
             And mountains, around whose towering summits the winds
             Of Heaven untrammelled flow--which air to breathe
             Is Happiness now, and will be Freedom hereafter
             In days that are to come?

Pol.   Oh, wilt thou--wilt thou
             Fly to that Paradise--my Lalage, wilt thou
             Fly thither with me? There Care shall be forgotten,
             And Sorrow shall be no more, and Eros be all.
             And life shall then be mine, for I will live
             For thee, and in thine eyes--and thou shalt be
             No more a mourner--but the radiant Joys
             Shall wait upon thee, and the angel Hope
             Attend thee ever; and I will kneel to thee
             And worship thee, and call thee my beloved,
             My own, my beautiful, my love, my wife,
             My all;--oh, wilt thou--wilt thou, Lalage,
             Fly thither with me?

Lal.   A deed is to be done--
             Castiglione lives!

Pol.   And he shall die!

       (Exit.)

Lal.
(after a pause). And--he--shall--die!--alas!
                Castiglione die? Who spoke the words?
                Where am I?--what was it he said?--Politian!
                Thou art not gone--thou art not gone, Politian!
                I feel thou art not gone--yet dare not look,
                Lest I behold thee not--thou couldst not go
                With those words upon thy lips--oh, speak to me!
                And let me hear thy voice--one word--one word,
                To say thou art not gone,--one little sentence,
                To say how thou dost scorn--how thou dost hate
                My womanly weakness. Ha! ha! thou art not gone--
                Oh, speak to me! I knew thou wouldst not go!
                I knew thou wouldst not, couldst not, durst not go.
                Villain, thou art not gone--thou mockest me!
                And thus I clutch thee--thus!--He is gone, he is gone--
                Gone--gone. Where am I?--'tis well--'tis very well!
                So that the blade be keen--the blow be sure,
                'Tis well, 'tis very well--alas! alas!

V.

The Suburbs. POLITIAN alone.

Politian. This weakness grows upon me. I am fain
                And much I fear me ill--it will not do
                To die ere I have lived!--Stay--stay thy hand,
                O Azrael, yet awhile!--Prince of the Powers
                Of Darkness and the Tomb, oh, pity me!
                Oh, pity me! let me not perish now,
                In the budding of my Paradisal Hope!
                Give me to live yet--yet a little while:
                'Tis I who pray for life--I who so late
                Demanded but to die!--What sayeth the Count?

        Enter Baldazzar.

Baldazzar.   That, knowing no cause of quarrel or of feud
                Between the Earl Politian and himself,
                He doth decline your cartel.

Pol.   What didst thou say?
                What answer was it you brought me, good Baldazzar?
                With what excessive fragrance the zephyr comes
                Laden from yonder bowers!--a fairer day,
                Or one more worthy Italy, methinks
                No mortal eyes have seen!--what said the Count?

Bal.   That he, Castiglione, not being aware
           Of any feud existing, or any cause
           Of quarrel between your lordship and himself,
           Cannot accept the challenge.

Pol.   It is most true--
           All this is very true. When saw you, sir,
           When saw you now, Baldazzar, in the frigid
           Ungenial Britain which we left so lately,
           A heaven so calm as this--so utterly free
           From the evil taint of clouds?--and he did say?

Bal.   No more, my lord, than I have told you:
           The Count Castiglione will not fight.
           Having no cause for quarrel.

Pol.   Now this is true--
           All very true. Thou art my friend, Baldazzar,
           And I have not forgotten it--thou'lt do me
           A piece of service: wilt thou go back and say
           Unto this man, that I, the Earl of Leicester,
           Hold him a villain?--thus much, I pr'ythee, say
           Unto the Count--it is exceeding just
           He should have cause for quarrel.

Bal.   My lord!--my friend!--

Pol. *(aside).* 'Tis he--he comes himself!
    (aloud.) Thou reasonest well.
           I know what thou wouldst say--not send the message--
           Well!--I will think of it--I will not send it.
           Now pr'ythee, leave me--hither doth come a person
           With whom affairs of a most private nature
           I would adjust.

Bal.   I go--to-morrow we meet,
           Do we not?--at the Vatican.

Pol.   At the Vatican.

      (Exit Bal.)

           Enter Castiglione.

Cas.   The Earl of Leicester here!

Pol.   I am the Earl of Leicester, and thou seest,
           Dost thou not, that I am here?

Cas.　　My lord, some strange,
　　　　　Some singular mistake--misunderstanding--
　　　　　Hath without doubt arisen: thou hast been urged
　　　　　Thereby, in heat of anger, to address
　　　　　Some words most unaccountable, in writing,
　　　　　To me, Castiglione; the bearer being
　　　　　Baldazzar, Duke of Surrey. I am aware
　　　　　Of nothing which might warrant thee in this thing,
　　　　　Having given thee no offence. Ha!--am I right?
　　　　　'Twas a mistake?--undoubtedly--we all
　　　　　Do err at times.

Pol.　　Draw, villain, and prate no more!

Cas.　　Ha!--draw?--and villain? have at thee then at once,
　　　　　Proud Earl!

　　　　(Draws.)

Pol.
(drawing.)　　Thus to the expiatory tomb,
　　　　　Untimely sepulchre, I do devote thee
　　　　　In the name of Lalage!

Cas. *(letting fall his sword and recoiling to the extremity of the stage.)*
　　　　　Of Lalage!
　　　　　Hold off--thy sacred hand!--avaunt, I say!
　　　　　Avaunt--I will not fight thee--indeed I dare not.

Pol.　　Thou wilt not fight with me didst say, Sir Count?
　　　　　Shall I be baffled thus?--now this is well;
　　　　　Didst say thou darest not? Ha!

Cas.　　I dare not--dare not--
　　　　　Hold off thy hand--with that beloved name
　　　　　So fresh upon thy lips I will not fight thee--
　　　　　I cannot--dare not.

Pol.　　Now, by my halidom,
　　　　　I do believe thee!--coward, I do believe thee!

Cas.　　Ha!--coward!--this may not be!

(clutches his sword and staggers towards Politian, but his purpose is changed before reaching him, and he falls upon hia knee at the feet of the Earl.)
　　　　　Alas! my lord,
　　　　　It is--it is--most true. In such a cause
　　　　　I am the veriest coward. Oh, pity me!

Pol.	
(greatly softened). Alas!--I do--indeed I pity thee.

Cas.	And Lalage--

Pol.	Scoundrel!--arise and die!

Cas.	It needeth not be--thus--thus--Oh, let me die
    Thus on my bended knee. It were most fitting
    That in this deep humiliation I perish.
    For in the fight I will not raise a hand
    Against thee, Earl of Leicester. Strike thou home--
  (baring his bosom.)
    Here is no let or hindrance to thy weapon--
    Strike home. I will not fight thee.

Pol.	Now's Death and Hell!
    Am I not--am I not sorely--grievously tempted
    To take thee at thy word? But mark me, sir:
    Think not to fly me thus. Do thou prepare
    For public insult in the streets--before
    The eyes of the citizens. I'll follow thee--
    Like an avenging spirit I'll follow thee
    Even unto death. Before those whom thou lovest--
    Before all Rome I'll taunt thee, villain,--I'll taunt thee,
    Dost hear? with cowardice--thou wilt not fight me?
    Thou liest! thou shalt!

    (Exit.)

Cas.	Now this indeed is just!
    Most righteous, and most just, avenging Heaven!

Footnotes:
1. By Sir Thomas Wyatt.--Ed.

NOTE ON POLITIAN

20. Such portions of "Politian" as are known to the public first saw the light of publicity in the 'Southern Literary Messenger' for December 1835 and January 1836, being styled "Scenes from Politian; an unpublished drama." These scenes were included, unaltered, in the 1845 collection of Poems by Poe. The larger portion of the original draft subsequently became the property of the present editor, but it is not considered just to the poet's memory to publish it. The work is a hasty and unrevised production of its author's earlier days of literary labor; and, beyond the scenes already known, scarcely calculated to enhance his reputation. As a specimen, however, of the parts unpublished, the following fragment from the first scene of Act II. may be offered. The Duke, it should be premised, is uncle to Alessandra, and father of Castiglione her betrothed.

Duke.   Why do you laugh?

Castiglione. Indeed.
              I hardly know myself. Stay! Was it not
              On yesterday we were speaking of the Earl?
              Of the Earl Politian? Yes! it was yesterday.
              Alessandra, you and I, you must remember!
              We were walking in the garden.

Duke.   Perfectly.
              I do remember it--what of it--what then?

Cas.   O nothing--nothing at all.

Duke.   Nothing at all!
              It is most singular that you should laugh
              At nothing at all!

Cas.   Most singular--singular!

Duke.   Look yon, Castiglione, be so kind
              As tell me, sir, at once what 'tis you mean.
              What are you talking of?

Cas.   Was it not so?
              We differed in opinion touching him.

Duke.   Him!--Whom?

Cas.   Why, sir, the Earl Politian.

Duke.   The Earl of Leicester! Yes!--is it he you mean?
             We differed, indeed. If I now recollect
             The words you used were that the Earl you knew
             Was neither learned nor mirthful.

Cas.   Ha! ha!--now did I?

Duke.   That did you, sir, and well I knew at the time
             You were wrong, it being not the character
             Of the Earl--whom all the world allows to be
             A most hilarious man. Be not, my son,
             Too positive again.

Cas.   'Tis singular!
             Most singular! I could not think it possible
             So little time could so much alter one!
             To say the truth about an hour ago,
             As I was walking with the Count San Ozzo,
             All arm in arm, we met this very man
             The Earl--he, with his friend Baldazzar,
             Having just arrived in Rome. Ha! ha! he is altered!
             Such an account he gave me of his journey!
             'Twould have made you die with laughter--such tales he
                told
             Of his caprices and his merry freaks
             Along the road--such oddity--such humor--
             Such wit--such whim--such flashes of wild merriment
             Set off too in such full relief by the grave
             Demeanor of his friend--who, to speak the truth
             Was gravity itself--

Duke.   Did I not tell you?

Cas.   You did--and yet 'tis strange! but true, as strange,
             How much I was mistaken! I always thought
             The Earl a gloomy man.

Duke.   So, so, you see!
             Be not too positive. Whom have we here?
             It cannot be the Earl?

Cas.   The Earl! Oh no!
             Tis not the Earl--but yet it is--and leaning
             Upon his friend Baldazzar. Ah! welcome, sir!

(Enter Politian and Baldazzar.)

                    My lord, a second welcome let me give you
                    To Rome--his Grace the Duke of Broglio.
                    Father! this is the Earl Politian, Earl
                    Of Leicester in Great Britain.

          [Politian bows haughtily.]

                    That, his friend
                    Baldazzar, Duke of Surrey. The Earl has letters,
                    So please you, for Your Grace.

Duke.   Ha! ha! Most welcome
                    To Rome and to our palace, Earl Politian!
                    And you, most noble Duke! I am glad to see you!
                    I knew your father well, my Lord Politian.
                    Castiglione! call your cousin hither,
                    And let me make the noble Earl acquainted
                    With your betrothed. You come, sir, at a time
                    Most seasonable. The wedding--

Politian. Touching those letters, sir,
                    Your son made mention of--your son, is he not?--
                    Touching those letters, sir, I wot not of them.
                    If such there be, my friend Baldazzar here--
                    Baldazzar! ah!--my friend Baldazzar here
                    Will hand them to Your Grace. I would retire.

Duke.   Retire!--so soon?

Cas.   What ho! Benito! Rupert!
                    His lordship's chambers--show his lordship to them!
                    His lordship is unwell.

          (Enter Benito.)

Ben.   This way, my lord!

          (Exit, followed by Politian.)

Duke.   Retire! Unwell!

Bal.   So please you, sir. I fear me
                    'Tis as you say--his lordship is unwell.
                    The damp air of the evening--the fatigue
                    Of a long journey--the--indeed I had better
                    Follow his lordship. He must be unwell.
                    I will return anon.

Duke.   Return anon!
        Now this is very strange! Castiglione!
        This way, my son, I wish to speak with thee.
        You surely were mistaken in what you said
        Of the Earl, mirthful, indeed!--which of us said
        Politian was a melancholy man?

   (Exeunt.)

POEMS OF YOUTH

INTRODUCTION TO POEMS—1831

LETTER TO MR. B--.
 "WEST POINT, 1831
 "DEAR B--
 ..
 Believing only a portion of my former volume to be worthy a second edition--that small portion I thought it as well to include in the present book as to republish by itself. I have therefore herein combined 'Al Aaraaf' and 'Tamerlane' with other poems hitherto unprinted. Nor have I hesitated to insert from the 'Minor Poems,' now omitted, whole lines, and even passages, to the end that being placed in a fairer light, and the trash shaken from them in which they were imbedded, they may have some chance of being seen by posterity.

 "It has been said that a good critique on a poem may be written by one who is no poet himself. This, according to your idea and mine of poetry, I feel to be false--the less poetical the critic, the less just the critique, and the converse. On this account, and because there are but few B----s in the world, I would be as much ashamed of the world's good opinion as proud of your own. Another than yourself might here observe, 'Shakespeare is in possession of the world's good opinion, and yet Shakespeare is the greatest of poets. It appears then that the world judge correctly, why should you be ashamed of their favorable judgment?' The difficulty lies in the interpretation of the word 'judgment' or 'opinion.' The opinion is the world's, truly, but it may be called theirs as a man would call a book his, having bought it; he did not write the book, but it is his; they did not originate the opinion, but it is theirs. A fool, for example, thinks Shakespeare a great poet--yet the fool has never read Shakespeare. But the fool's neighbor, who is a step higher on the Andes of the mind, whose head (that is to say, his more exalted thought) is too far above the fool to be seen or understood, but whose feet (by which I mean his every-day actions) are sufficiently near to be discerned, and by means of which that superiority is ascertained, which but for them would never have been discovered--this neighbor asserts that Shakespeare is a great poet--the fool believes him, and it is henceforward his opinion. This neighbor's own opinion has, in like manner, been adopted from one above him, and so, ascendingly, to a few gifted individuals who kneel around the summit, beholding, face to face, the master spirit who stands upon the pinnacle.

 "You are aware of the great barrier in the path of an American writer. He is read, if at all, in preference to the combined and established wit of the world. I say established; for it is with literature as with law or empire--an established name is an estate in tenure, or a throne in possession. Besides, one might suppose that books, like their authors, improve by travel--their having crossed the sea is, with us, so great a distinction. Our antiquaries abandon time for distance; our very fops glance from the binding to the bottom of the title-page, where the mystic characters which spell London, Paris, or Genoa, are precisely so many letters of recommendation.

"I mentioned just now a vulgar error as regards criticism. I think the notion that no poet can form a correct estimate of his own writings is another. I remarked before that in proportion to the poetical talent would be the justice of a critique upon poetry. Therefore a bad poet would, I grant, make a false critique, and his self-love would infallibly bias his little judgment in his favor; but a poet, who is indeed a poet, could not, I think, fail of making a just critique; whatever should be deducted on the score of self-love might be replaced on account of his intimate acquaintance with the subject; in short, we have more instances of false criticism than of just where one's own writings are the test, simply because we have more bad poets than good. There are, of course, many objections to what I say: Milton is a great example of the contrary; but his opinion with respect to the 'Paradise Regained' is by no means fairly ascertained. By what trivial circumstances men are often led to assert what they do not really believe! Perhaps an inadvertent word has descended to posterity. But, in fact, the 'Paradise Regained' is little, if at all, inferior to the 'Paradise Lost,' and is only supposed so to be because men do not like epics, whatever they may say to the contrary, and reading those of Milton in their natural order, are too much wearied with the first to derive any pleasure from the second.

"I dare say Milton preferred 'Comus' to either--if so--justly.

"As I am speaking of poetry, it will not be amiss to touch slightly upon the most singular heresy in its modern history--the heresy of what is called, very foolishly, the Lake School. Some years ago I might have been induced, by an occasion like the present, to attempt a formal refutation of their doctrine; at present it would be a work of supererogation. The wise must bow to the wisdom of such men as Coleridge and Southey, but being wise, have laughed at poetical theories so prosaically exemplified.

"Aristotle, with singular assurance, has declared poetry the most philosophical of all writings--but it required a Wordsworth to pronounce it the most metaphysical. He seems to think that the end of poetry is, or should be, instruction; yet it is a truism that the end of our existence is happiness; if so, the end of every separate part of our existence, everything connected with our existence, should be still happiness. Therefore the end of instruction should be happiness; and happiness is another name for pleasure;--therefore the end of instruction should be pleasure: yet we see the above-mentioned opinion implies precisely the reverse.

"To proceed: ceteris paribus, he who pleases is of more importance to his fellow-men than he who instructs, since utility is happiness, and pleasure is the end already obtained which instruction is merely the means of obtaining.

"I see no reason, then, why our metaphysical poets should plume themselves so much on the utility of their works, unless indeed they refer to instruction with eternity in view; in which case, sincere respect for their piety would not allow me to express my contempt for their judgment; contempt which it would be difficult to conceal, since their writings are professedly to be understood by the few, and it is the many who stand in need of salvation. In such case I should no doubt be tempted to think of the devil in 'Melmoth,' who labors indefatigably, through three octavo volumes, to accomplish the destruction of one or two souls, while any common devil would have demolished one or two thousand.

"Against the subtleties which would make poetry a study--not a passion--it becomes the metaphysician to reason--but the poet to protest. Yet Wordsworth and Coleridge are men in years; the one imbued in contemplation from his childhood; the other a giant in intellect and learning. The diffidence, then, with which I venture to dispute their authority would be overwhelming did I not feel, from the bottom of my heart, that learning has little to do with the imagination--intellect with the passions--or age with poetry.

"'Trifles, like straws, upon the surface flow;
He who would search for pearls must dive below,'

"are lines which have done much mischief. As regards the greater truths, men oftener err by seeking them at the bottom than at the top; Truth lies in the huge abysses where wisdom is sought--not in the palpable palaces where she is found. The ancients were not always right in hiding the goddess in a well; witness the light which Bacon has thrown upon philosophy; witness the principles of our divine faith--that moral mechanism by which the simplicity of a child may overbalance the wisdom of a man.

"We see an instance of Coleridge's liability to err, in his 'Biographia Literaria'--professedly his literary life and opinions, but, in fact, a treatise 'de omni scibili et quibusdam aliis'. He goes wrong by reason of his very profundity, and of his error we have a natural type in the contemplation of a star. He who regards it directly and intensely sees, it is true, the star, but it is the star without a ray--while he who surveys it less inquisitively is conscious of all for which the star is useful to us below--its brilliancy and its beauty.

"As to Wordsworth, I have no faith in him. That he had in youth the feelings of a poet I believe--for there are glimpses of extreme delicacy in his writings--(and delicacy is the poet's own kingdom--his 'El Dorado')--but they have the appearance of a better day recollected; and glimpses, at best, are little evidence of present poetic fire; we know that a few straggling flowers spring up daily in the crevices of the glacier.

"He was to blame in wearing away his youth in contemplation with the end of poetizing in his manhood. With the increase of his judgment the light which should make it apparent has faded away. His judgment consequently is too correct. This may not be understood,--but the old Goths of Germany would have understood it, who used to debate matters of importance to their State twice, once when drunk, and once when sober--sober that they might not be deficient in formality--drunk lest they should be destitute of vigor.

"The long wordy discussions by which he tries to reason us into admiration of his poetry, speak very little in his favor: they are full of such assertions as this (I have opened one of his volumes at random)--'Of genius the only proof is the act of doing well what is worthy to be done, and what was never done before;'--indeed? then it follows that in doing what is 'un'worthy to be done, or what 'has' been done before, no genius can be evinced; yet the picking of pockets is an unworthy act, pockets have been picked time immemorial, and

Barrington, the pick-pocket, in point of genius, would have thought hard of a comparison with William Wordsworth, the poet.

"Again, in estimating the merit of certain poems, whether they be Ossian's or Macpherson's can surely be of little consequence, yet, in order to prove their worthlessness, Mr. W. has expended many pages in the controversy. 'Tantænæ animis?' Can great minds descend to such absurdity? But worse still: that he may bear down every argument in favor of these poems, he triumphantly drags forward a passage, in his abomination with which he expects the reader to sympathise. It is the beginning of the epic poem 'Temora.' 'The blue waves of Ullin roll in light; the green hills are covered with day; trees shake their dusty heads in the breeze.' And this--this gorgeous, yet simple imagery, where all is alive and panting with immortality--this, William Wordsworth, the author of 'Peter Bell,' has 'selected' for his contempt. We shall see what better he, in his own person, has to offer. Imprimis:

> *"'And now she's at the pony's tail,*
> *And now she's at the pony's head,*
> *On that side now, and now on this;*
> *And, almost stifled with her bliss,*
> *A few sad tears does Betty shed....*
> *She pats the pony, where or when*
> *She knows not ... happy Betty Foy!*
> *Oh, Johnny, never mind the doctor!'*

"Secondly:

> *"'The dew was falling fast, the--stars began to blink;*
> *I heard a voice: it said,--"Drink, pretty creature, drink!"*
> *And, looking o'er the hedge, before me I espied*
> *A snow-white mountain lamb, with a maiden at its side.*
> *No other sheep was near, the lamb was all alone,*
> *And by a slender cord was tether'd to a stone.'*

"Now, we have no doubt this is all true: we will believe it, indeed we will, Mr, W. Is it sympathy for the sheep you wish to excite? I love a sheep from the bottom of my heart.

"But there are occasions, dear B----, there are occasions when even Wordsworth is reasonable. Even Stamboul, it is said, shall have an end, and the most unlucky blunders must come to a conclusion. Here is an extract from his preface:

"'Those who have been accustomed to the phraseology of modern writers, if they persist in reading this book to a conclusion (impossible!) will, no doubt, have to struggle with feelings of awkwardness; (ha! ha! ha!) they will look round for poetry (ha! ha! ha! ha!), and will be induced to inquire by what species of courtesy these attempts have been permitted to assume that title.' Ha! ha! ha! ha! ha!

"Yet, let not Mr. W. despair; he has given immortality to a wagon, and the bee Sophocles has transmitted to eternity a sore toe, and dignified a tragedy with a chorus of turkeys.

"Of Coleridge, I cannot speak but with reverence. His towering intellect! his gigantic power! To use an author quoted by himself,

'J'ai trouvé souvent que la plupart des sectes ont raison dans une bonne partie de ce qu'elles avancent, mais non pas en ce qu'elles nient;'

and to employ his own language, he has imprisoned his own conceptions by the barrier he has erected against those of others. It is lamentable to think that such a mind should be buried in metaphysics, and, like the Nyctanthes, waste its perfume upon the night alone. In reading that man's poetry, I tremble like one who stands upon a volcano, conscious from the very darkness bursting from the crater, of the fire and the light that are weltering below.

"What is Poetry?--Poetry! that Proteus-like idea, with as many appellations as the nine-titled Corcyra! 'Give me,' I demanded of a scholar some time ago, 'give me a definition of poetry.' 'Tres-volontiers;' and he proceeded to his library, brought me a Dr. Johnson, and overwhelmed me with a definition. Shade of the immortal Shakespeare! I imagine to myself the scowl of your spiritual eye upon the profanity of that scurrilous Ursa Major. Think of poetry, dear B----, think of poetry, and then think of Dr. Samuel Johnson! Think of all that is airy and fairy-like, and then of all that is hideous and unwieldy; think of his huge bulk, the Elephant! and then--and then think of the 'Tempest'--the 'Midsummer Night's Dream'--Prospero--Oberon--and Titania!

"A poem, in my opinion, is opposed to a work of science by having, for its immediate object, pleasure, not truth; to romance, by having, for its object, an indefinite instead of a definite pleasure, being a poem only so far as this object is attained; romance presenting perceptible images with definite, poetry with indefinite sensations, to which end music is an essential, since the comprehension of sweet sound is our most indefinite conception. Music, when combined with a pleasurable idea, is poetry; music, without the idea, is simply music; the idea, without the music, is prose, from its very definitiveness.

"What was meant by the invective against him who had no music in his soul?

"To sum up this long rigmarole, I have, dear B----, what you, no doubt, perceive, for the metaphysical poets as poets, the most sovereign contempt. That they have followers proves nothing:

> "'No Indian prince has to his palace
> More followers than a thief to the gallows.'"

SONNET---TO SCIENCE

SCIENCE! true daughter of Old Time thou art!
    Who alterest all things with thy peering eyes.
Why preyest thou thus upon the poet's heart,
    Vulture, whose wings are dull realities
How should he love thee? or how deem thee wise,
    Who wouldst not leave him in his wandering
To seek for treasure in the jewelled skies,
    Albeit he soared with an undaunted wing!
Hast thou not dragged Diana from her car?
    And driven the Hamadryad from the wood
To seek a shelter in some happier star?
    Hast thou not torn the Naiad from her flood,
The Elfin from the green grass, and from me
The summer dream beneath the tamarind tree?

1829.

Private reasons--some of which have reference to the sin of plagiarism, and others to the date of Tennyson's first poems[1]--have induced me, after some hesitation, to republish these, the crude compositions of my earliest boyhood. They are printed 'verbatim'--without alteration from the original edition--the date of which is too remote to be judiciously acknowledged.--E. A. P. (1845).

Footnotes:

1. This refers to the accusation brought against Edgar Poe that he was a copyist of Tennyson.--Ed.

AL AARAAF[1]

PART I

O! nothing earthly save the ray
(Thrown back from flowers) of Beauty's eye,
As in those gardens where the day
Springs from the gems of Circassy--
O! nothing earthly save the thrill
Of melody in woodland rill--
Or (music of the passion-hearted)
Joy's voice so peacefully departed
That like the murmur in the shell,
Its echo dwelleth and will dwell--
O! nothing of the dross of ours--
Yet all the beauty--all the flowers
That list our Love, and deck our bowers--
Adorn yon world afar, afar--
The wandering star.

'Twas a sweet time for Nesace--for there
Her world lay lolling on the golden air,
Near four bright suns--a temporary rest--
An oasis in desert of the blest.
Away away--'mid seas of rays that roll
Empyrean splendor o'er th' unchained soul--
The soul that scarce (the billows are so dense)
Can struggle to its destin'd eminence--
To distant spheres, from time to time, she rode,
And late to ours, the favour'd one of God--
But, now, the ruler of an anchor'd realm,
She throws aside the sceptre--leaves the helm,
And, amid incense and high spiritual hymns,
Laves in quadruple light her angel limbs.

Now happiest, loveliest in yon lovely Earth,
Whence sprang the "Idea of Beauty" into birth,
(Falling in wreaths thro' many a startled star,
Like woman's hair 'mid pearls, until, afar,
It lit on hills Achaian, and there dwelt),
She look'd into Infinity--and knelt.
Rich clouds, for canopies, about her curled--
Fit emblems of the model of her world--
Seen but in beauty--not impeding sight--

Of other beauty glittering thro' the light--
A wreath that twined each starry form around,
And all the opal'd air in color bound.

All hurriedly she knelt upon a bed
Of flowers: of lilies such as rear'd the head
On the fair Capo Deucato [2], and sprang
So eagerly around about to hang
Upon the flying footsteps of--deep pride--
Of her who lov'd a mortal--and so died [3].
The Sephalica, budding with young bees,
Uprear'd its purple stem around her knees:
And gemmy flower, of Trebizond misnam'd [4]--
Inmate of highest stars, where erst it sham'd
All other loveliness: its honied dew
(The fabled nectar that the heathen knew)
Deliriously sweet, was dropp'd from Heaven,
And fell on gardens of the unforgiven
In Trebizond--and on a sunny flower
So like its own above that, to this hour,
It still remaineth, torturing the bee
With madness, and unwonted reverie:
In Heaven, and all its environs, the leaf
And blossom of the fairy plant, in grief
Disconsolate linger--grief that hangs her head,
Repenting follies that full long have fled,
Heaving her white breast to the balmy air,
Like guilty beauty, chasten'd, and more fair:
Nyctanthes too, as sacred as the light
She fears to perfume, perfuming the night:
And Clytia [5] pondering between many a sun,
While pettish tears adown her petals run:
And that aspiring flower that sprang on Earth [6]--
And died, ere scarce exalted into birth,
Bursting its odorous heart in spirit to wing
Its way to Heaven, from garden of a king:
And Valisnerian lotus thither flown [7]
From struggling with the waters of the Rhone:
And thy most lovely purple perfume, Zante [8]!
Isola d'oro!--Fior di Levante!
And the Nelumbo bud that floats for ever [9]
With Indian Cupid down the holy river--
Fair flowers, and fairy! to whose care is given
To bear the Goddess' song, in odors, up to Heaven [10]:

    "Spirit! that dwellest where,
     In the deep sky,
    The terrible and fair,
     In beauty vie!
    Beyond the line of blue--

    The boundary of the star
    Which turneth at the view
     Of thy barrier and thy bar--
    Of the barrier overgone
     By the comets who were cast
    From their pride, and from their throne
     To be drudges till the last--
    To be carriers of fire
     (The red fire of their heart)
    With speed that may not tire
     And with pain that shall not part--
    Who livest--that we know--
     In Eternity--we feel--
    But the shadow of whose brow
     What spirit shall reveal?
    Tho' the beings whom thy Nesace,
     Thy messenger hath known
    Have dream'd for thy Infinity
     A model of their own [11]--
    Thy will is done, O God!
     The star hath ridden high
    Thro' many a tempest, but she rode
     Beneath thy burning eye;
    And here, in thought, to thee--
     In thought that can alone
    Ascend thy empire and so be
     A partner of thy throne--
    By winged Fantasy [12],
    My embassy is given,
    Till secrecy shall knowledge be
     In the environs of Heaven."

She ceas'd--and buried then her burning cheek
Abash'd, amid the lilies there, to seek
A shelter from the fervor of His eye;
For the stars trembled at the Deity.
She stirr'd not--breath'd not--for a voice was there
How solemnly pervading the calm air!
A sound of silence on the startled ear
Which dreamy poets name "the music of the sphere."
Ours is a world of words: Quiet we call
"Silence"--which is the merest word of all.

All Nature speaks, and ev'n ideal things
Flap shadowy sounds from the visionary wings--
But ah! not so when, thus, in realms on high
The eternal voice of God is passing by,
And the red winds are withering in the sky!
"What tho' in worlds which sightless cycles run [13],
Link'd to a little system, and one sun--

Where all my love is folly, and the crowd
Still think my terrors but the thunder cloud,
The storm, the earthquake, and the ocean-wrath
(Ah! will they cross me in my angrier path?)
What tho' in worlds which own a single sun
The sands of time grow dimmer as they run,
Yet thine is my resplendency, so given
To bear my secrets thro' the upper Heaven.
Leave tenantless thy crystal home, and fly,
With all thy train, athwart the moony sky--
Apart--like fire-flies in Sicilian night [14],
And wing to other worlds another light!
Divulge the secrets of thy embassy
To the proud orbs that twinkle--and so be
To ev'ry heart a barrier and a ban
Lest the stars totter in the guilt of man!"

Up rose the maiden in the yellow night,
The single-mooned eve!-on earth we plight
Our faith to one love--and one moon adore--
The birth-place of young Beauty had no more.
As sprang that yellow star from downy hours,
Up rose the maiden from her shrine of flowers,
And bent o'er sheeny mountain and dim plain
Her way--but left not yet her Therasæan reign [15].

PART II

High on a mountain of enamell'd head--
Such as the drowsy shepherd on his bed
Of giant pasturage lying at his ease,
Raising his heavy eyelid, starts and sees
With many a mutter'd "hope to be forgiven"
What time the moon is quadrated in Heaven--
Of rosy head, that towering far away
Into the sunlit ether, caught the ray
Of sunken suns at eve--at noon of night,
While the moon danc'd with the fair stranger light--
Uprear'd upon such height arose a pile
Of gorgeous columns on th' uuburthen'd air,
Flashing from Parian marble that twin smile
Far down upon the wave that sparkled there,
And nursled the young mountain in its lair.
Of molten stars their pavement, such as fall [16]
Thro' the ebon air, besilvering the pall
Of their own dissolution, while they die--
Adorning then the dwellings of the sky.
A dome, by linked light from Heaven let down,
Sat gently on these columns as a crown--
A window of one circular diamond, there,

Look'd out above into the purple air
And rays from God shot down that meteor chain
And hallow'd all the beauty twice again,
Save when, between th' Empyrean and that ring,
Some eager spirit flapp'd his dusky wing.
But on the pillars Seraph eyes have seen
The dimness of this world: that grayish green
That Nature loves the best for Beauty's grave
Lurk'd in each cornice, round each architrave--
And every sculptured cherub thereabout
That from his marble dwelling peered out,
Seem'd earthly in the shadow of his niche--
Achaian statues in a world so rich?
Friezes from Tadmor and Persepolis [17]--
From Balbec, and the stilly, clear abyss
Of beautiful Gomorrah! Oh, the wave [18]
Is now upon thee--but too late to save!
Sound loves to revel in a summer night:
Witness the murmur of the gray twilight
That stole upon the ear, in Eyraco [19],
Of many a wild star-gazer long ago--
That stealeth ever on the ear of him
Who, musing, gazeth on the distance dim,
And sees the darkness coming as a cloud--
Is not its form--its voice--most palpable and loud?[20]
 But what is this?--it cometh--and it brings
A music with it--'tis the rush of wings--
A pause--and then a sweeping, falling strain,
And Nesace is in her halls again.
From the wild energy of wanton haste
Her cheeks were flushing, and her lips apart;
The zone that clung around her gentle waist
Had burst beneath the heaving of her heart.
Within the centre of that hall to breathe
She paus'd and panted, Zanthe! all beneath,
The fairy light that kiss'd her golden hair
And long'd to rest, yet could but sparkle there!

Young flowers were whispering in melody [21]
To happy flowers that night--and tree to tree;
Fountains were gushing music as they fell
In many a star-lit grove, or moon-light dell;
Yet silence came upon material things--
Fair flowers, bright waterfalls and angel wings--
And sound alone that from the spirit sprang
Bore burthen to the charm the maiden sang:

    "Neath blue-bell or streamer--
     Or tufted wild spray
    That keeps, from the dreamer,

The moonbeam away--[22]
Bright beings! that ponder,
 With half-closing eyes,
On the stars which your wonder
 Hath drawn from the skies,
Till they glance thro' the shade, and
 Come down to your brow
Like--eyes of the maiden
 Who calls on you now--
Arise! from your dreaming
 In violet bowers,
To duty beseeming
 These star-litten hours--
And shake from your tresses
 Encumber'd with dew

The breath of those kisses
 That cumber them too--
(O! how, without you, Love!
 Could angels be blest?)
Those kisses of true love
 That lull'd ye to rest!
Up! shake from your wing
 Each hindering thing:
The dew of the night--
 It would weigh down your flight;
And true love caresses--
 O! leave them apart!
They are light on the tresses,
 But lead on the heart.

Ligeia! Ligeia!
 My beautiful one!
Whose harshest idea
 Will to melody run,
O! is it thy will
 On the breezes to toss?
Or, capriciously still,
 Like the lone Albatross, [23]
Incumbent on night
 (As she on the air)
To keep watch with delight
 On the harmony there?

Ligeia! wherever
 Thy image may be,
No magic shall sever
 Thy music from thee.
Thou hast bound many eyes
 In a dreamy sleep--

But the strains still arise
  Which thy vigilance keep--

The sound of the rain
  Which leaps down to the flower,
And dances again
  In the rhythm of the shower--
The murmur that springs [24]
  From the growing of grass
Are the music of things--
  But are modell'd, alas!
Away, then, my dearest,
  O! hie thee away
To springs that lie clearest
  Beneath the moon-ray--
To lone lake that smiles,
  In its dream of deep rest,
At the many star-isles
That enjewel its breast--
Where wild flowers, creeping,
  Have mingled their shade,
On its margin is sleeping
  Full many a maid--
Some have left the cool glade, and
  Have slept with the bee--[25]
Arouse them, my maiden,
  On moorland and lea--

Go! breathe on their slumber,
  All softly in ear,
The musical number
  They slumber'd to hear--
For what can awaken
  An angel so soon
Whose sleep hath been taken
  Beneath the cold moon,
As the spell which no slumber
  Of witchery may test,
The rhythmical number
  Which lull'd him to rest?"

Spirits in wing, and angels to the view,
A thousand seraphs burst th' Empyrean thro',
Young dreams still hovering on their drowsy flight--
Seraphs in all but "Knowledge," the keen light
That fell, refracted, thro' thy bounds afar,
O death! from eye of God upon that star;
Sweet was that error--sweeter still that death--
Sweet was that error--ev'n with us the breath
Of Science dims the mirror of our joy--

To them 'twere the Simoom, and would destroy--
For what (to them) availeth it to know
That Truth is Falsehood--or that Bliss is Woe?
Sweet was their death--with them to die was rife
With the last ecstasy of satiate life--
Beyond that death no immortality--
But sleep that pondereth and is not "to be"--
And there--oh! may my weary spirit dwell--
Apart from Heaven's Eternity--and yet how far from Hell! [26]

What guilty spirit, in what shrubbery dim
Heard not the stirring summons of that hymn?
But two: they fell: for heaven no grace imparts
To those who hear not for their beating hearts.
A maiden-angel and her seraph-lover--
O! where (and ye may seek the wide skies over)
Was Love, the blind, near sober Duty known?
Unguided Love hath fallen--'mid "tears of perfect moan." [27]

He was a goodly spirit--he who fell:
A wanderer by mossy-mantled well--
A gazer on the lights that shine above--
A dreamer in the moonbeam by his love:
What wonder? for each star is eye-like there,
And looks so sweetly down on Beauty's hair--
And they, and ev'ry mossy spring were holy
To his love-haunted heart and melancholy.
The night had found (to him a night of wo)
Upon a mountain crag, young Angelo--
Beetling it bends athwart the solemn sky,
And scowls on starry worlds that down beneath it lie.
Here sate he with his love--his dark eye bent
With eagle gaze along the firmament:
Now turn'd it upon her--but ever then
It trembled to the orb of EARTH again.

"Ianthe, dearest, see! how dim that ray!
How lovely 'tis to look so far away!
She seemed not thus upon that autumn eve
I left her gorgeous halls--nor mourned to leave,
That eve--that eve--I should remember well--
The sun-ray dropped, in Lemnos with a spell
On th' Arabesque carving of a gilded hall
Wherein I sate, and on the draperied wall--
And on my eyelids--O, the heavy light!
How drowsily it weighed them into night!
On flowers, before, and mist, and love they ran
With Persian Saadi in his Gulistan:
But O, that light!--I slumbered--Death, the while,
Stole o'er my senses in that lovely isle

So softly that no single silken hair
Awoke that slept--or knew that he was there.

"The last spot of Earth's orb I trod upon
Was a proud temple called the Parthenon; [28]
More beauty clung around her columned wall
Then even thy glowing bosom beats withal, [29]
And when old Time my wing did disenthral
Thence sprang I--as the eagle from his tower,
And years I left behind me in an hour.
What time upon her airy bounds I hung,
One half the garden of her globe was flung
Unrolling as a chart unto my view--
Tenantless cities of the desert too!
Ianthe, beauty crowded on me then,
And half I wished to be again of men."

"My Angelo! and why of them to be?
A brighter dwelling-place is here for thee--
And greener fields than in yon world above,
And woman's loveliness--and passionate love."
"But list, Ianthe! when the air so soft
Failed, as my pennoned spirit leapt aloft, [30]
Perhaps my brain grew dizzy--but the world
I left so late was into chaos hurled,
Sprang from her station, on the winds apart,
And rolled a flame, the fiery Heaven athwart.
Methought, my sweet one, then I ceased to soar,
And fell--not swiftly as I rose before,
But with a downward, tremulous motion thro'
Light, brazen rays, this golden star unto!
Nor long the measure of my falling hours,
For nearest of all stars was thine to ours--
Dread star! that came, amid a night of mirth,
A red Daedalion on the timid Earth."

"We came--and to thy Earth--but not to us
Be given our lady's bidding to discuss:
We came, my love; around, above, below,
Gay fire-fly of the night we come and go,
Nor ask a reason save the angel-nod
She grants to us as granted by her God--
But, Angelo, than thine gray Time unfurled
Never his fairy wing o'er fairer world!
Dim was its little disk, and angel eyes
Alone could see the phantom in the skies,
When first Al Aaraaf knew her course to be
Headlong thitherward o'er the starry sea--
But when its glory swelled upon the sky,
As glowing Beauty's bust beneath man's eye,

We paused before the heritage of men,
And thy star trembled--as doth Beauty then!"

Thus in discourse, the lovers whiled away
The night that waned and waned and brought no day.
They fell: for Heaven to them no hope imparts
Who hear not for the beating of their hearts.

1839.

Footnotes:

1. A star was discovered by Tycho Brahe which appeared suddenly in the heavens--attained, in a few days, a brilliancy surpassing that of Jupiter--then as suddenly disappeared, and has never been seen since.

2. On Santa Maura--olim Deucadia.

3. Sappho.

4. This flower is much noticed by Lewenhoeck and Tournefort. The bee, feeding upon its blossom, becomes intoxicated.

5. Clytia--the Chrysanthemum Peruvianum, or, to employ a better-known term, the turnsol--which turns continually towards the sun, covers itself, like Peru, the country from which it comes, with dewy clouds which cool and refresh its flowers during the most violent heat of the day.--'B. de St. Pierre.'

6. There is cultivated in the king's garden at Paris, a species of serpentine aloe without prickles, whose large and beautiful flower exhales a strong odor of the vanilla, during the time of its expansion, which is very short. It does not blow till towards the month of July--you then perceive it gradually open its petals—expand them--fade and die.--'St. Pierre'.

7. There is found, in the Rhone, a beautiful lily of the Valisnerian kind. Its stem will stretch to the length of three or four feet--thus preserving its head above water in the swellings of the river.

8. The Hyacinth.

9. It is a fiction of the Indians, that Cupid was first seen floating in one of these down the river Ganges, and that he still loves the cradle of his childhood.

10. And golden vials full of odors which are the prayers of the saints.--'Rev. St. John.'

11. The Humanitarians held that God was to be understood as having really a human form.--'Vide Clarke's Sermons', vol. I, page 26, fol. edit.

The drift of Milton's argument leads him to employ language which would appear, at first sight, to verge upon their doctrine; but it will be seen immediately, that he guards himself against the charge of having adopted one of the most ignorant errors of the dark ages of the Church.--'Dr. Sumner's Notes on Milton's Christian Doctrine'.

This opinion, in spite of many testimonies to the contrary, could never have been very general. Andeus, a Syrian of Mesopotamia, was condemned for the opinion, as heretical. He lived in the beginning of the fourth century. His disciples were called Anthropomorphites.--'Vide du Pin'.

Among Milton's minor poems are these lines:

Dicite sacrorum præsides nemorum Dese, etc.,
Quis ille primus cujus ex imagine
Natura solers finxit humanum genus?
Eternus, incorruptus, æquævus polo,
Unusque et universus exemplar Dei.

--And afterwards,

Non cui profundum Cæcitas lumen dedit
Dircæus augur vidit hunc alto sinu, etc.

    12. Seltsamen Tochter Jovis
Seinem Schosskinde
Der Phantasie.
    'Goethe'.
    13. Sightless--too small to be seen.--'Legge'.
    14. I have often noticed a peculiar movement of the fire-flies; they will collect in a body and fly off, from a common centre, into innumerable radii.
    15. Therasæa, or Therasea, the island mentioned by Seneca, which, in a moment, arose from the sea to the eyes of astonished mariners.
    16. Some star which, from the ruin'd roof
Of shak'd Olympus, by mischance did fall.
    'Milton'.
    17. Voltaire, in speaking of Persepolis, says,
    "Je connais bien l'admiration qu'inspirent ces ruines--mais un palais érigé au pied d'une chaîne de rochers steriles--peut-il être un chef d'oeuvre des arts!"
    18. "Oh, the wave"--Ula Deguisi is the Turkish appellation; but, on its own shores, it is called Baliar Loth, or Al-motanah. There were undoubtedly more than two cities engulphed in the "dead sea." In the valley of Siddim were five-- Adrah, Zeboin, Zoar, Sodom and Gomorrah. Stephen of Byzantium mentions eight, and Strabo thirteen (engulphed) --but the last is out of all reason. It is said (Tacitus, Strabo, Josephus, Daniel of St. Saba, Nau, Maundrell, Troilo, D'Arvieux), that after an excessive drought, the vestiges of columns, walls, etc., are seen above the surface. At 'any' season, such remains may be discovered by looking down into the transparent lake, and at such distance as would argue the existence of many settlements in the space now usurped by the "Asphaltites."
    19. Eyraco-Chaldea.
    20. I have often thought I could distinctly hear the sound of the darkness as it stole over the horizon.
    21. Fairies use flowers for their charactery.
    'Merry Wives of Windsor'.
    22. In Scripture is this passage:

"The sun shall not harm thee by day, nor the moon by night."

    It is, perhaps, not generally known that the moon, in Egypt, has the effect of producing blindness to those who sleep with the face exposed to its rays, to which circumstances the passage evidently alludes.
    23. The Albatross is said to sleep on the wing.
    24. I met with this idea in an old English tale, which I am now unable to obtain and quote from memory:

"The verie essence and, as it were, springe heade and origine of all musiche is the verie pleasaunte sounde which the trees of the forest do make when they growe."

25. The wild bee will not sleep in the shade if there be moonlight. The rhyme in the verse, as in one about sixty lines before, has an appearance of affectation. It is, however, imitated from Sir W. Scott, or rather from Claud Halcro--in whose mouth I admired its effect:

O! were there an island,
    Tho' ever so wild,
Where woman might smile, and
    No man be beguil'd, etc.

26. With the Arabians there is a medium between Heaven and Hell, where men suffer no punishment, but yet do not attain that tranquil and even happiness which they suppose to be characteristic of heavenly enjoyment.

Un no rompido sueno--
Un dia puro--allegre--libre
Quiera--
Libre de amor--de zelo--
De odio--de esperanza--de rezelo.

'Luis Ponce de Leon.'

Sorrow is not excluded from "Al Aaraaf," but it is that sorrow which the living love to cherish for the dead, and which, in some minds, resembles the delirium of opium.

The passionate excitement of Love and the buoyancy of spirit attendant upon intoxication are its less holy pleasures--the price of which, to those souls who make choice of "Al Aaraaf" as their residence after life, is final death and annihilation.

27. There be tears of perfect moan
Wept for thee in Helicon.
    'Milton'.
28. It was entire in 1687--the most elevated spot in Athens.
29. Shadowing more beauty in their airy brows
Than have the white breasts of the queen of love.
    'Marlowe.'
30. Pennon, for pinion.--'Milton'.

TAMERLANE

Kind solace in a dying hour!
Such, father, is not (now) my theme--
I will not madly deem that power
Of Earth may shrive me of the sin
Unearthly pride hath revelled in--
I have no time to dote or dream:
You call it hope--that fire of fire!
It is but agony of desire:
If I can hope--O God! I can--
Its fount is holier--more divine--
I would not call thee fool, old man,
But such is not a gift of thine.

Know thou the secret of a spirit
Bowed from its wild pride into shame
O yearning heart! I did inherit
Thy withering portion with the fame,
The searing glory which hath shone
Amid the Jewels of my throne,
Halo of Hell! and with a pain
Not Hell shall make me fear again--
O craving heart, for the lost flowers
And sunshine of my summer hours!
The undying voice of that dead time,
With its interminable chime,
Rings, in the spirit of a spell,
Upon thy emptiness--a knell.

I have not always been as now:
The fevered diadem on my brow
I claimed and won usurpingly--
Hath not the same fierce heirdom given
Rome to the Cæsar--this to me?
The heritage of a kingly mind,
And a proud spirit which hath striven
Triumphantly with human kind.
On mountain soil I first drew life:
The mists of the Taglay have shed
Nightly their dews upon my head,
And, I believe, the winged strife
And tumult of the headlong air
Have nestled in my very hair.

Edgar Allan Poe

So late from Heaven--that dew--it fell
('Mid dreams of an unholy night)
Upon me with the touch of Hell,
While the red flashing of the light
From clouds that hung, like banners, o'er,
Appeared to my half-closing eye
The pageantry of monarchy;
And the deep trumpet-thunder's roar
Came hurriedly upon me, telling
Of human battle, where my voice,
My own voice, silly child!--was swelling
(O! how my spirit would rejoice,
And leap within me at the cry)
The battle-cry of Victory!

The rain came down upon my head
Unsheltered--and the heavy wind
Rendered me mad and deaf and blind.
It was but man, I thought, who shed
Laurels upon me: and the rush--
The torrent of the chilly air
Gurgled within my ear the crush
Of empires--with the captive's prayer--
The hum of suitors--and the tone
Of flattery 'round a sovereign's throne.

My passions, from that hapless hour,
Usurped a tyranny which men
Have deemed since I have reached to power,
My innate nature--be it so:
But, father, there lived one who, then,
Then--in my boyhood--when their fire
Burned with a still intenser glow
(For passion must, with youth, expire)
E'en then who knew this iron heart
In woman's weakness had a part.

I have no words--alas!--to tell
The loveliness of loving well!
Nor would I now attempt to trace
The more than beauty of a face
Whose lineaments, upon my mind,
Are--shadows on th' unstable wind:
Thus I remember having dwelt
Some page of early lore upon,
With loitering eye, till I have felt
The letters--with their meaning--melt
To fantasies--with none.

O, she was worthy of all love!
Love as in infancy was mine--
'Twas such as angel minds above
Might envy; her young heart the shrine
On which my every hope and thought
Were incense--then a goodly gift,
For they were childish and upright--
Pure--as her young example taught:
Why did I leave it, and, adrift,
Trust to the fire within, for light?

We grew in age--and love--together--
Roaming the forest, and the wild;
My breast her shield in wintry weather--
And, when the friendly sunshine smiled.
And she would mark the opening skies,
I saw no Heaven--but in her eyes.
Young Love's first lesson is----the heart:
For 'mid that sunshine, and those smiles,
When, from our little cares apart,
And laughing at her girlish wiles,
I'd throw me on her throbbing breast,
And pour my spirit out in tears--
There was no need to speak the rest--
No need to quiet any fears
Of her--who asked no reason why,
But turned on me her quiet eye!

Yet more than worthy of the love
My spirit struggled with, and strove
When, on the mountain peak, alone,
Ambition lent it a new tone--
I had no being--but in thee:
The world, and all it did contain
In the earth--the air--the sea--
Its joy--its little lot of pain
That was new pleasure--the ideal,
Dim, vanities of dreams by night--
And dimmer nothings which were real--
(Shadows--and a more shadowy light!)
Parted upon their misty wings,
And, so, confusedly, became
Thine image and--a name--a name!
Two separate--yet most intimate things.

I was ambitious--have you known
The passion, father? You have not:
A cottager, I marked a throne
Of half the world as all my own,
And murmured at such lowly lot--

Edgar Allan Poe

But, just like any other dream,
Upon the vapor of the dew
My own had past, did not the beam
Of beauty which did while it thro'
The minute--the hour--the day--oppress
My mind with double loveliness.

We walked together on the crown
Of a high mountain which looked down
Afar from its proud natural towers
Of rock and forest, on the hills--
The dwindled hills! begirt with bowers
And shouting with a thousand rills.

I spoke to her of power and pride,
But mystically--in such guise
That she might deem it nought beside
The moment's converse; in her eyes
I read, perhaps too carelessly--
A mingled feeling with my own--
The flush on her bright cheek, to me
Seemed to become a queenly throne
Too well that I should let it be
Light in the wilderness alone.

I wrapped myself in grandeur then,
And donned a visionary crown--
Yet it was not that Fantasy
Had thrown her mantle over me--
But that, among the rabble--men,
Lion ambition is chained down--
And crouches to a keeper's hand--
Not so in deserts where the grand--
The wild--the terrible conspire
With their own breath to fan his fire.

Look 'round thee now on Samarcand!--
Is she not queen of Earth? her pride
Above all cities? in her hand
Their destinies? in all beside
Of glory which the world hath known
Stands she not nobly and alone?
Falling--her veriest stepping-stone
Shall form the pedestal of a throne--
And who her sovereign? Timour--he
Whom the astonished people saw
Striding o'er empires haughtily
A diademed outlaw!

O, human love! thou spirit given,
On Earth, of all we hope in Heaven!
Which fall'st into the soul like rain
Upon the Siroc-withered plain,
And, failing in thy power to bless,
But leav'st the heart a wilderness!
Idea! which bindest life around
With music of so strange a sound
And beauty of so wild a birth--
Farewell! for I have won the Earth.

When Hope, the eagle that towered, could see
No cliff beyond him in the sky,
His pinions were bent droopingly--
And homeward turned his softened eye.
'Twas sunset: When the sun will part
There comes a sullenness of heart
To him who still would look upon
The glory of the summer sun.
That soul will hate the ev'ning mist
So often lovely, and will list
To the sound of the coming darkness (known
To those whose spirits hearken) as one
Who, in a dream of night, would fly,
But cannot, from a danger nigh.

What tho' the moon--tho' the white moon
Shed all the splendor of her noon,
Her smile is chilly--and her beam,
In that time of dreariness, will seem
(So like you gather in your breath)
A portrait taken after death.
And boyhood is a summer sun
Whose waning is the dreariest one--
For all we live to know is known,
And all we seek to keep hath flown--
Let life, then, as the day-flower, fall
With the noon-day beauty--which is all.
I reached my home--my home no more--
For all had flown who made it so.
I passed from out its mossy door,
And, tho' my tread was soft and low,
A voice came from the threshold stone
Of one whom I had earlier known--
O, I defy thee, Hell, to show
On beds of fire that burn below,
An humbler heart--a deeper woe.

Father, I firmly do believe--
I know--for Death who comes for me
From regions of the blest afar,
Where there is nothing to deceive,
Hath left his iron gate ajar.
And rays of truth you cannot see
Are flashing thro' Eternity----
I do believe that Eblis hath
A snare in every human path--
Else how, when in the holy grove
I wandered of the idol, Love,--
Who daily scents his snowy wings
With incense of burnt-offerings
From the most unpolluted things,
Whose pleasant bowers are yet so riven
Above with trellised rays from Heaven
No mote may shun--no tiniest fly--
The light'ning of his eagle eye--
How was it that Ambition crept,
Unseen, amid the revels there,
Till growing bold, he laughed and leapt
In the tangles of Love's very hair!

   1829.

TO HELEN

Helen, thy beauty is to me
    Like those Nicean barks of yore,
That gently, o'er a perfumed sea,
    The weary, wayworn wanderer bore
    To his own native shore.

On desperate seas long wont to roam,
    Thy hyacinth hair, thy classic face,
Thy Naiad airs have brought me home
    To the glory that was Greece,
To the grandeur that was Rome.

Lo! in yon brilliant window niche,
    How statue-like I see thee stand,
    The agate lamp within thy hand!
Ah, Psyche, from the regions which
    Are Holy Land!

1831.

THE VALLEY OF UNREST

Once it smiled a silent dell
Where the people did not dwell;
They had gone unto the wars,
Trusting to the mild-eyed stars,
Nightly, from their azure towers,
To keep watch above the flowers,
In the midst of which all day
The red sun-light lazily lay,
Now each visitor shall confess
The sad valley's restlessness.
Nothing there is motionless--
Nothing save the airs that brood
Over the magic solitude.
Ah, by no wind are stirred those trees
That palpitate like the chill seas
Around the misty Hebrides!
Ah, by no wind those clouds are driven
That rustle through the unquiet Heaven
Unceasingly, from morn till even,
Over the violets there that lie
In myriad types of the human eye--
Over the lilies that wave
And weep above a nameless grave!
They wave:--from out their fragrant tops
Eternal dews come down in drops.
They weep:--from off their delicate stems
Perennial tears descend in gems.

    1831.

ISRAFEL[1]

In Heaven a spirit doth dwell
    "Whose heart-strings are a lute;"
None sing so wildly well
As the angel Israfel,
And the giddy Stars (so legends tell),
Ceasing their hymns, attend the spell
    Of his voice, all mute.

Tottering above
    In her highest noon,
    The enamoured Moon
Blushes with love,
    While, to listen, the red levin
    (With the rapid Pleiads, even,
    Which were seven),
    Pauses in Heaven.

And they say (the starry choir
    And the other listening things)
That Israfeli's fire
Is owing to that lyre
    By which he sits and sings--
The trembling living wire
Of those unusual strings.

But the skies that angel trod,
    Where deep thoughts are a duty--
Where Love's a grow-up God--
    Where the Houri glances are
Imbued with all the beauty
    Which we worship in a star.

Therefore, thou art not wrong,
    Israfeli, who despisest
An unimpassioned song;
To thee the laurels belong,
    Best bard, because the wisest!
Merrily live and long!

The ecstasies above
    With thy burning measures suit--
Thy grief, thy joy, thy hate, thy love,

With the fervor of thy lute--
Well may the stars be mute!

Yes, Heaven is thine; but this
   Is a world of sweets and sours;
   Our flowers are merely--flowers,
And the shadow of thy perfect bliss
   Is the sunshine of ours.

If I could dwell
Where Israfel
   Hath dwelt, and he where I,
He might not sing so wildly well
   A mortal melody,
While a bolder note than this might swell
   From my lyre within the sky.

1836.

Footnotes:

1. And the angel Israfel, whose heart-strings are a lute, and who has the sweetest voice of all God's creatures.
'Koran'.

TO———

I heed not that my earthly lot
    Hath--little of Earth in it--
That years of love have been forgot
    In the hatred of a minute:--
I mourn not that the desolate
    Are happier, sweet, than I,
But that you sorrow for my fate
    Who am a passer-by.

1829.

TO----

The bowers whereat, in dreams, I see
    The wantonest singing birds,

Are lips--and all thy melody
    Of lip-begotten words--

Thine eyes, in Heaven of heart enshrined
    Then desolately fall,
O God! on my funereal mind
    Like starlight on a pall--

Thy heart--thy heart!--I wake and sigh,
    And sleep to dream till day
Of the truth that gold can never buy--
    Of the baubles that it may.

    1829.

TO THE RIVER

Fair river! in thy bright, clear flow
    Of crystal, wandering water,
Thou art an emblem of the glow
    Of beauty--the unhidden heart--
    The playful maziness of art
    In old Alberto's daughter;

But when within thy wave she looks--
    Which glistens then, and trembles--
Why, then, the prettiest of brooks
    Her worshipper resembles;
For in his heart, as in thy stream,
    Her image deeply lies--
His heart which trembles at the beam
    Of her soul-searching eyes.

1829.

SONG

I saw thee on thy bridal day--
    When a burning blush came o'er thee,
Though happiness around thee lay,
    The world all love before thee:

And in thine eye a kindling light
    (Whatever it might be)
Was all on Earth my aching sight
    Of Loveliness could see.

That blush, perhaps, was maiden shame--
    As such it well may pass--
Though its glow hath raised a fiercer flame
    In the breast of him, alas!

Who saw thee on that bridal day,
    When that deep blush would come o'er thee,
Though happiness around thee lay,
    The world all love before thee.

    1827.

SPIRITS OF THE DEAD

Thy soul shall find itself alone
'Mid dark thoughts of the gray tombstone
Not one, of all the crowd, to pry
Into thine hour of secrecy.
Be silent in that solitude
    Which is not loneliness--for then
The spirits of the dead who stood
    In life before thee are again
In death around thee--and their will
Shall overshadow thee: be still.
The night--tho' clear--shall frown--
And the stars shall not look down
From their high thrones in the Heaven,
With light like Hope to mortals given--
But their red orbs, without beam,
To thy weariness shall seem
As a burning and a fever
Which would cling to thee forever.
Now are thoughts thou shalt not banish--
Now are visions ne'er to vanish--
From thy spirit shall they pass
No more--like dew-drops from the grass.
The breeze--the breath of God--is still--
And the mist upon the hill
Shadowy--shadowy--yet unbroken,
    Is a symbol and a token--
    How it hangs upon the trees,
    A mystery of mysteries!

1837.

A DREAM

In visions of the dark night
    I have dreamed of joy departed--
But a waking dream of life and light
    Hath left me broken-hearted.

Ah! what is not a dream by day
    To him whose eyes are cast
On things around him with a ray
    Turned back upon the past?

That holy dream--that holy dream,
    While all the world were chiding,
Hath cheered me as a lovely beam,
    A lonely spirit guiding.

What though that light, thro' storm and night,
    So trembled from afar--
What could there be more purely bright
    In Truth's day star?

1837.

ROMANCE

Romance, who loves to nod and sing,
With drowsy head and folded wing,
Among the green leaves as they shake
Far down within some shadowy lake,
To me a painted paroquet
Hath been--a most familiar bird--
Taught me my alphabet to say--
To lisp my very earliest word
While in the wild wood I did lie,
A child--with a most knowing eye.

Of late, eternal Condor years
So shake the very Heaven on high
With tumult as they thunder by,
I have no time for idle cares
Though gazing on the unquiet sky.
And when an hour with calmer wings
Its down upon my spirit flings--
That little time with lyre and rhyme
To while away--forbidden things!
My heart would feel to be a crime
Unless it trembled with the strings.

    1829.

FAIRYLAND

Dim vales--and shadowy floods--
And cloudy-looking woods,
Whose forms we can't discover
For the tears that drip all over
Huge moons there wax and wane--
Again--again--again--
Every moment of the night--
Forever changing places--
And they put out the star-light
With the breath from their pale faces.
About twelve by the moon-dial
One more filmy than the rest
(A kind which, upon trial,
They have found to be the best)
Comes down--still down--and down
With its centre on the crown
Of a mountain's eminence,
While its wide circumference
In easy drapery falls
Over hamlets, over halls,
Wherever they may be--
O'er the strange woods--o'er the sea--
Over spirits on the wing--
Over every drowsy thing--
And buries them up quite
In a labyrinth of light--
And then, how deep!--O, deep!
Is the passion of their sleep.
In the morning they arise,
And their moony covering
Is soaring in the skies,
With the tempests as they toss,
Like--almost any thing--
Or a yellow Albatross.
They use that moon no more
For the same end as before--
Videlicet a tent--
Which I think extravagant:
Its atomies, however,
Into a shower dissever,
Of which those butterflies,
Of Earth, who seek the skies,

The Complete Poetical Works of Edgar Allan Poe
And so come down again
(Never-contented thing!)
Have brought a specimen
Upon their quivering wings.

   1831.

THE LAKE

In spring of youth it was my lot
To haunt of the wide world a spot
The which I could not love the less--
So lovely was the loneliness
Of a wild lake, with black rock bound,
And the tall pines that towered around.

But when the Night had thrown her pall
Upon the spot, as upon all,
And the mystic wind went by
Murmuring in melody--
Then--ah, then, I would awake
To the terror of the lone lake.

Yet that terror was not fright,
But a tremulous delight--
A feeling not the jewelled mine
Could teach or bribe me to define--
Nor Love--although the Love were thine.

Death was in that poisonous wave,
And in its gulf a fitting grave
For him who thence could solace bring
To his lone imagining--
Whose solitary soul could make
An Eden of that dim lake.

    1827.

EVENING STAR

'Twas noontide of summer,
    And midtime of night,
And stars, in their orbits,
    Shone pale, through the light
Of the brighter, cold moon.
    'Mid planets her slaves,
Herself in the Heavens,
    Her beam on the waves.

    I gazed awhile
    On her cold smile;
Too cold--too cold for me--
    There passed, as a shroud,
    A fleecy cloud,
And I turned away to thee,
    Proud Evening Star,
    In thy glory afar
And dearer thy beam shall be;
    For joy to my heart
    Is the proud part
Thou bearest in Heaven at night,
    And more I admire
    Thy distant fire,
Than that colder, lowly light.

    1827.

IMITATION

A dark unfathomed tide
Of interminable pride--
A mystery, and a dream,
Should my early life seem;
I say that dream was fraught
With a wild and waking thought
Of beings that have been,
Which my spirit hath not seen,
Had I let them pass me by,
With a dreaming eye!
Let none of earth inherit
That vision on my spirit;
Those thoughts I would control,
As a spell upon his soul:
For that bright hope at last
And that light time have past,
And my wordly rest hath gone
With a sigh as it passed on:
I care not though it perish
With a thought I then did cherish.

1827.

"THE HAPPIEST DAY"

I. The happiest day--the happiest hour
    My seared and blighted heart hath known,
    The highest hope of pride and power,
    I feel hath flown.

II. Of power! said I? Yes! such I ween
    But they have vanished long, alas!
    The visions of my youth have been--
    But let them pass.

III. And pride, what have I now with thee?
    Another brow may ev'n inherit
    The venom thou hast poured on me--
    Be still my spirit!

IV. The happiest day--the happiest hour
    Mine eyes shall see--have ever seen
    The brightest glance of pride and power
    I feel have been:

V. But were that hope of pride and power
    Now offered with the pain
    Ev'n then I felt--that brightest hour
    I would not live again:

VI. For on its wing was dark alloy
    And as it fluttered--fell
    An essence--powerful to destroy
    A soul that knew it well.

1827.

Translation from the Greek

HYMN TO ARISTOGEITON AND HARMODIUS

I.   Wreathed in myrtle, my sword I'll conceal,
        Like those champions devoted and brave,
        When they plunged in the tyrant their steel,
        And to Athens deliverance gave.

II.   Beloved heroes! your deathless souls roam
        In the joy breathing isles of the blest;
        Where the mighty of old have their home--
        Where Achilles and Diomed rest.

III.   In fresh myrtle my blade I'll entwine,
        Like Harmodius, the gallant and good,
        When he made at the tutelar shrine
        A libation of Tyranny's blood.

IV.   Ye deliverers of Athens from shame!
        Ye avengers of Liberty's wrongs!
        Endless ages shall cherish your fame,
        Embalmed in their echoing songs!

1827

DREAMS

Oh! that my young life were a lasting dream!
My spirit not awakening, till the beam
Of an Eternity should bring the morrow.
Yes! though that long dream were of hopeless sorrow,
'Twere better than the cold reality
Of waking life, to him whose heart must be,
And hath been still, upon the lovely earth,
A chaos of deep passion, from his birth.
But should it be--that dream eternally
Continuing--as dreams have been to me
In my young boyhood--should it thus be given,
'Twere folly still to hope for higher Heaven.
For I have revelled when the sun was bright
I' the summer sky, in dreams of living light
And loveliness,--have left my very heart
Inclines of my imaginary apart[1]
From mine own home, with beings that have been
Of mine own thought--what more could I have seen?
'Twas once--and only once--and the wild hour
From my remembrance shall not pass--some power
Or spell had bound me--'twas the chilly wind
Came o'er me in the night, and left behind
Its image on my spirit--or the moon
Shone on my slumbers in her lofty noon
Too coldly--or the stars--howe'er it was
That dream was that that night-wind--let it pass.
I have been happy, though in a dream.
I have been happy--and I love the theme:
Dreams! in their vivid coloring of life
As in that fleeting, shadowy, misty strife
Of semblance with reality which brings
To the delirious eye, more lovely things
Of Paradise and Love--and all my own!--
Than young Hope in his sunniest hour hath known.

Footnotes:

    1. In climes of mine imagining apart?--Ed.

Edgar Allan Poe

"IN YOUTH I HAVE KNOWN ONE."

        How often we forget all time, when lone
        Admiring Nature's universal throne;
        Her woods--her wilds--her mountains--the intense
        Reply of Hers to Our intelligence!

I.   In youth I have known one with whom the Earth
        In secret communing held--as he with it,
        In daylight, and in beauty, from his birth:
        Whose fervid, flickering torch of life was lit
        From the sun and stars, whence he had drawn forth
        A passionate light such for his spirit was fit--
        And yet that spirit knew--not in the hour
        Of its own fervor--what had o'er it power.

II.   Perhaps it may be that my mind is wrought
        To a ferver[1] by the moonbeam that hangs o'er,
        But I will half believe that wild light fraught
        With more of sovereignty than ancient lore
        Hath ever told--or is it of a thought
        The unembodied essence, and no more
        That with a quickening spell doth o'er us pass
        As dew of the night-time, o'er the summer grass?

III. Doth o'er us pass, when, as th' expanding eye
        To the loved object--so the tear to the lid
        Will start, which lately slept in apathy?
        And yet it need not be--(that object) hid
        From us in life--but common--which doth lie
        Each hour before us--but then only bid
        With a strange sound, as of a harp-string broken
        T' awake us--'Tis a symbol and a token--

IV. Of what in other worlds shall be--and given
        In beauty by our God, to those alone
        Who otherwise would fall from life and Heaven
        Drawn by their heart's passion, and that tone,

That high tone of the spirit which hath striven
Though not with Faith--with godliness--whose throne
With desperate energy 't hath beaten down;
Wearing its own deep feeling as a crown.

Footnotes:

1. Query "fervor"?--Ed.

A PÆAN

I.   How shall the burial rite be read?
        The solemn song be sung?
        The requiem for the loveliest dead,
        That ever died so young?

II.   Her friends are gazing on her,
        And on her gaudy bier,
        And weep!--oh! to dishonor
        Dead beauty with a tear!

III. They loved her for her wealth--
        And they hated her for her pride--
        But she grew in feeble health,
        And they love her--that she died.

IV. They tell me (while they speak
        Of her "costly broider'd pall")
        That my voice is growing weak--
        That I should not sing at all--

V.   Or that my tone should be
        Tun'd to such solemn song
        So mournfully--so mournfully,
        That the dead may feel no wrong.

VI. But she is gone above,
        With young Hope at her side,
        And I am drunk with love
        Of the dead, who is my bride.--

VII. Of the dead--dead who lies
        All perfum'd there,
        With the death upon her eyes.
        And the life upon her hair.

VIII.   Thus on the coffin loud and long
        I strike--the murmur sent
        Through the gray chambers to my song,
        Shall be the accompaniment.

IX.   Thou diedst in thy life's June--
        But thou didst not die too fair:
        Thou didst not die too soon,
        Nor with too calm an air.

X.   From more than friends on earth,
        Thy life and love are riven,
        To join the untainted mirth
        Of more than thrones in heaven.--

XI.   Therefore, to thee this night
        I will no requiem raise,
        But waft thee on thy flight,
        With a Pæan of old days.

NOTES

30. On the "Poems written in Youth" little comment is needed. This section includes the pieces printed for the first volume of 1827 (which was subsequently suppressed), such poems from the first and second published volumes of 1829 and 1831 as have not already been given in their revised versions, and a few others collected from various sources.

"Al Aaraaf" first appeared, with the sonnet "To Silence" prefixed to it, in 1829, and is, substantially, as originally issued. In the edition for 1831, however, this poem, its author's longest, was introduced by the following twenty-nine lines, which have been omitted in all subsequent collections:

AL AARAAF

Mysterious star!
Thou wert my dream
All a long summer night--
Be now my theme!
By this clear stream,
Of thee will I write;
Meantime from afar
Bathe me in light!

Thy world has not the dross of ours,
Yet all the beauty--all the flowers
That list our love or deck our bowers
In dreamy gardens, where do lie
Dreamy maidens all the day;
While the silver winds of Circassy
On violet couches faint away.
Little--oh! little dwells in thee
Like unto what on earth we see:
Beauty's eye is here the bluest
In the falsest and untruest--
On the sweetest air doth float
The most sad and solemn note--
If with thee be broken hearts,
Joy so peacefully departs,
That its echo still doth dwell,
Like the murmur in the shell.
Thou! thy truest type of grief
Is the gently falling leaf--
Thou! thy framing is so holy

Sorrow is not melancholy.

31. The earliest version of "Tamerlane" was included in the suppressed volume of 1827, but differs very considerably from the poem as now published. The present draft, besides innumerable verbal alterations and improvements upon the original, is more carefully punctuated, and, the lines being indented, presents a more pleasing appearance, to the eye at least.

32. "To Helen" first appeared in the 1831 volume, as did also "The Valley of Unrest" (as "The Valley Nis"), "Israfel," and one or two others of the youthful pieces.

The poem styled "Romance" constituted the Preface of the 1829 volume, but with the addition of the following lines:

Succeeding years, too wild for song,
Then rolled like tropic storms along,
Where, though the garish lights that fly
Dying along the troubled sky,
Lay bare, through vistas thunder-riven,
The blackness of the general Heaven,
That very blackness yet doth fling
Light on the lightning's silver wing.

For being an idle boy lang syne,
Who read Anacreon and drank wine,
I early found Anacreon rhymes
Were almost passionate sometimes--
And by strange alchemy of brain
His pleasures always turned to pain--
His naïveté to wild desire--
His wit to love--his wine to fire--
And so, being young and dipt in folly,
I fell in love with melancholy.

And used to throw my earthly rest
And quiet all away in jest--
I could not love except where Death
Was mingling his with Beauty's breath--
Or Hymen, Time, and Destiny,
Were stalking between her and me.

* * * * *

But now my soul hath too much room--
Gone are the glory and the gloom--
The black hath mellow'd into gray,
And all the fires are fading away.

My draught of passion hath been deep--
I revell'd, and I now would sleep--
And after drunkenness of soul

Edgar Allan Poe

Succeeds the glories of the bowl--
An idle longing night and day
To dream my very life away.

But dreams--of those who dream as I,
Aspiringly, are damned, and die:
Yet should I swear I mean alone,
By notes so very shrilly blown,
To break upon Time's monotone,
While yet my vapid joy and grief
Are tintless of the yellow leaf--
Why not an imp the greybeard hath,
Will shake his shadow in my path--
And e'en the greybeard will o'erlook
Connivingly my dreaming-book.

DOUBTFUL POEMS

ALONE

From childhood's hour I have not been
As others were--I have not seen
As others saw--I could not bring
My passions from a common spring--
From the same source I have not taken
My sorrow--I could not awaken
My heart to joy at the same tone--
And all I loved--I loved alone--
Thou--in my childhood--in the dawn
Of a most stormy life--was drawn
From every depth of good and ill
The mystery which binds me still--
From the torrent, or the fountain--
From the red cliff of the mountain--
From the sun that round me roll'd
In its autumn tint of gold--
From the lightning in the sky
As it passed me flying by--
From the thunder and the storm--
And the cloud that took the form
(When the rest of Heaven was blue)
Of a demon in my view.

    March 17, 1829.

Edgar Allan Poe

TO ISADORE

I.   Beneath the vine-clad eaves,
     Whose shadows fall before
     Thy lowly cottage door--
   Under the lilac's tremulous leaves--
   Within thy snowy clasped hand
   The purple flowers it bore.
   Last eve in dreams, I saw thee stand,
   Like queenly nymph from Fairy-land--
   Enchantress of the flowery wand,
     Most beauteous Isadore!

II.   And when I bade the dream
     Upon thy spirit flee,
     Thy violet eyes to me
   Upturned, did overflowing seem
   With the deep, untold delight
     Of Love's serenity;
   Thy classic brow, like lilies white
   And pale as the Imperial Night
   Upon her throne, with stars bedight,
     Enthralled my soul to thee!

III.   Ah! ever I behold
     Thy dreamy, passionate eyes,
     Blue as the languid skies
   Hung with the sunset's fringe of gold;
   Now strangely clear thine image grows,
     And olden memories
   Are startled from their long repose
   Like shadows on the silent snows
   When suddenly the night-wind blows
     Where quiet moonlight lies.

IV.   Like music heard in dreams,
     Like strains of harps unknown,
     Of birds for ever flown,--
   Audible as the voice of streams
   That murmur in some leafy dell,
     I hear thy gentlest tone,
   And Silence cometh with her spell
   Like that which on my tongue doth dwell,
   When tremulous in dreams I tell

My love to thee alone!

V.   In every valley heard,
      Floating from tree to tree,
      Less beautiful to me,
    The music of the radiant bird,
    Than artless accents such as thine
      Whose echoes never flee!
    Ah! how for thy sweet voice I pine:--
    For uttered in thy tones benign
    (Enchantress!) this rude name of mine
      Doth seem a melody!

THE VILLAGE STREET

In these rapid, restless shadows,
    Once I walked at eventide,
When a gentle, silent maiden,
    Walked in beauty at my side.
She alone there walked beside me
All in beauty, like a bride.

Pallidly the moon was shining
    On the dewy meadows nigh;
On the silvery, silent rivers,
    On the mountains far and high,--
On the ocean's star-lit waters,
    Where the winds a-weary die.

Slowly, silently we wandered
    From the open cottage door,
Underneath the elm's long branches
    To the pavement bending o'er;
Underneath the mossy willow
    And the dying sycamore.

With the myriad stars in beauty
    All bedight, the heavens were seen,
Radiant hopes were bright around me,
    Like the light of stars serene;
Like the mellow midnight splendor
    Of the Night's irradiate queen.

Audibly the elm-leaves whispered
    Peaceful, pleasant melodies,
Like the distant murmured music
    Of unquiet, lovely seas;
While the winds were hushed in slumber
    In the fragrant flowers and trees.

Wondrous and unwonted beauty
    Still adorning all did seem,
While I told my love in fables
    'Neath the willows by the stream;
Would the heart have kept unspoken
    Love that was its rarest dream!

Instantly away we wandered
    In the shadowy twilight tide,
She, the silent, scornful maiden,
    Walking calmly at my side,
With a step serene and stately,
    All in beauty, all in pride.

Vacantly I walked beside her.
    On the earth mine eyes were cast;
Swift and keen there came unto me
    Bitter memories of the past--
On me, like the rain in Autumn
    On the dead leaves, cold and fast.

Underneath the elms we parted,
    By the lowly cottage door;
One brief word alone was uttered--
    Never on our lips before;
And away I walked forlornly,
Broken-hearted evermore.

Slowly, silently I loitered,
    Homeward, in the night, alone;
Sudden anguish bound my spirit,
    That my youth had never known;
Wild unrest, like that which cometh
    When the Night's first dream hath flown.

Now, to me the elm-leaves whisper
    Mad, discordant melodies,
And keen melodies like shadows
    Haunt the moaning willow trees,
And the sycamores with laughter
    Mock me in the nightly breeze.

Sad and pale the Autumn moonlight
    Through the sighing foliage streams;
And each morning, midnight shadow,
    Shadow of my sorrow seems;
Strive, O heart, forget thine idol!
    And, O soul, forget thy dreams!

Edgar Allan Poe

THE FOREST REVERIE

     'Tis said that when
     The hands of men
     Tamed this primeval wood,
And hoary trees with groans of wo,
Like warriors by an unknown foe,
     Were in their strength subdued,
     The virgin Earth
     Gave instant birth
     To springs that ne'er did flow--
     That in the sun
     Did rivulets run,
And all around rare flowers did blow--
     The wild rose pale
     Perfumed the gale,
And the queenly lily adown the dale
     (Whom the sun and the dew
     And the winds did woo),
With the gourd and the grape luxuriant grew.

     So when in tears
     The love of years
     Is wasted like the snow,
And the fine fibrils of its life
By the rude wrong of instant strife
     Are broken at a blow--
     Within the heart
     Do springs upstart
     Of which it doth now know,
     And strange, sweet dreams,
     Like silent streams
That from new fountains overflow,
     With the earlier tide
     Of rivers glide
Deep in the heart whose hope has died--
Quenching the fires its ashes hide,--
     Its ashes, whence will spring and grow
     Sweet flowers, ere long,--
     The rare and radiant flowers of song!

NOTES

Of the many verses from time to time ascribed to the pen of Edgar Poe, and not included among his known writings, the lines entitled "Alone" have the chief claim to our notice. 'Fac-simile' copies of this piece had been in possession of the present editor some time previous to its publication in 'Scribner's Magazine' for September 1875; but as proofs of the authorship claimed for it were not forthcoming, he refrained from publishing it as requested. The desired proofs have not yet been adduced, and there is, at present, nothing but internal evidence to guide us. "Alone" is stated to have been written by Poe in the album of a Baltimore lady (Mrs. Balderstone?), on March 17th, 1829, and the 'fac-simile' given in 'Scribner's' is alleged to be of his handwriting. If the caligraphy be Poe's, it is different in all essential respects from all the many specimens known to us, and strongly resembles that of the writer of the heading and dating of the manuscript, both of which the contributor of the poem acknowledges to have been recently added. The lines, however, if not by Poe, are the most successful imitation of his early mannerisms yet made public, and, in the opinion of one well qualified to speak, "are not unworthy on the whole of the parentage claimed for them."

Whilst Edgar Poe was editor of the 'Broadway Journal', some lines "To Isadore" appeared therein, and, like several of his known pieces, bore no signature. They were at once ascribed to Poe, and in order to satisfy questioners, an editorial paragraph subsequently appeared, saying they were by "A. Ide, junior." Two previous poems had appeared in the 'Broadway Journal' over the signature of "A. M. Ide," and whoever wrote them was also the author of the lines "To Isadore." In order, doubtless, to give a show of variety, Poe was then publishing some of his known works in his journal over 'noms de plume', and as no other writings whatever can be traced to any person bearing the name of "A. M. Ide," it is not impossible that the poems now republished in this collection may be by the author of "The Raven." Having been published without his usual elaborate revision, Poe may have wished to hide his hasty work under an assumed name. The three pieces are included in the present collection, so the reader can judge for himself what pretensions they possess to be by the author of "The Raven."

PROSE POEMS

THE ISLAND OF THE FAY

"Nullus enim locus sine genio est."
  Servius.

"La musique," says Marmontel, in those "Contes Moraux"[1] which in all our translations we have insisted upon calling "Moral Tales," as if in mockery of their spirit--"la musique est le seul des talens qui jouisse de lui-meme: tous les autres veulent des temoins." He here confounds the pleasure derivable from sweet sounds with the capacity for creating them. No more than any other talent, is that for music susceptible of complete enjoyment where there is no second party to appreciate its exercise; and it is only in common with other talents that it produces effects which may be fully enjoyed in solitude. The idea which the raconteur has either failed to entertain clearly, or has sacrificed in its expression to his national love of point, is doubtless the very tenable one that the higher order of music is the most thoroughly estimated when we are exclusively alone. The proposition in this form will be admitted at once by those who love the lyre for its own sake and for its spiritual uses. But there is one pleasure still within the reach of fallen mortality, and perhaps only one, which owes even more than does music to the accessory sentiment of seclusion. I mean the happiness experienced in the contemplation of natural scenery. In truth, the man who would behold aright the glory of God upon earth must in solitude behold that glory. To me at least the presence, not of human life only, but of life, in any other form than that of the green things which grow upon the soil and are voiceless, is a stain upon the landscape, is at war with the genius of the scene. I love, indeed, to regard the dark valleys, and the gray rocks, and the waters that silently smile, and the forests that sigh in uneasy slumbers, and the proud watchful mountains that look down upon all,--I love to regard these as themselves but the colossal members of one vast animate and sentient whole--a whole whose form (that of the sphere) is the most perfect and most inclusive of all; whose path is among associate planets; whose meek handmaiden is the moon; whose mediate sovereign is the sun; whose life is eternity; whose thought is that of a god; whose enjoyment is knowledge; whose destinies are lost in immensity; whose cognizance of ourselves is akin with our own cognizance of the animalculæ which infest the brain, a being which we in consequence regard as purely inanimate and material, much in the same manner as these animalculæ must thus regard us.

Our telescopes and our mathematical investigations assure us on every hand, notwithstanding the cant of the more ignorant of the priesthood, that space, and therefore that bulk, is an important consideration in the eyes of the Almighty.

The cycles in which the stars move are those best adapted for the evolution, without collision, of the greatest possible number of bodies. The forms of those bodies are accurately such as within a given surface to include the greatest possible amount of matter; while the surfaces themselves are so disposed as to accommodate a denser population than could be accommodated on the same surfaces otherwise arranged. Nor is it any argument against bulk being an object with God that space itself is infinite; for there may be an infinity of matter to fill it; and since we see clearly that the endowment of matter with vitality is a principle--indeed, as far as our judgments extend, the leading principle in the operations of Deity, it is scarcely logical to imagine it confined to the regions of the minute, where we daily trace it, and not extending to those of the august. As we find cycle within cycle without end, yet all revolving around one far-distant centre which is the Godhead, may we not analogically suppose, in the same manner, life within life, the less within the greater, and all within the Spirit Divine? In short, we are madly erring through self-esteem in believing man, in either his temporal or future destinies, to be of more moment in the universe than that vast "clod of the valley" which he tills and contemns, and to which he denies a soul, for no more profound reason than that he does not behold it in operation [2].

These fancies, and such as these, have always given to my meditations among the mountains and the forests, by the rivers and the ocean, a tinge of what the every-day world would not fail to term the fantastic. My wanderings amid such scenes have been many and far-searching, and often solitary; and the interest with which I have strayed through many a dim deep valley, or gazed into the reflected heaven of many a bright lake, has been an interest greatly deepened by the thought that I have strayed and gazed alone. What flippant Frenchman [3] was it who said, in allusion to the well known work of Zimmermann, that "la solitude est une belle chose; mais il faut quelqu'un pour vous dire que la solitude est une belle chose"? The epigram cannot be gainsaid; but the necessity is a thing that does not exist.

It was during one of my lonely journeyings, amid a far distant region of mountain locked within mountain, and sad rivers and melancholy tarns writhing or sleeping within all, that I chanced upon a certain rivulet and island. I came upon them suddenly in the leafy June, and threw myself upon the turf beneath the branches of an unknown odorous shrub, that I might doze as I contemplated the scene. I felt that thus only should I look upon it, such was the character of phantasm which it wore.

On all sides, save to the west where the sun was about sinking, arose the verdant walls of the forest. The little river which turned sharply in its course, and was thus immediately lost to sight, seemed to have no exit from its prison, but to be absorbed by the deep green foliage of the trees to the east; while in the opposite quarter (so it appeared to me as I lay at length and glanced upward) there poured down noiselessly and continuously into the valley a rich golden and crimson waterfall from the sunset fountains of the sky.

About midway in the short vista which my dreamy vision took in, one small circular island, profusely verdured, reposed upon the bosom of the stream.

Edgar Allan Poe

So blended bank and shadow there,
That each seemed pendulous in air--

so mirror-like was the glassy water, that it was scarcely possible to say at what point upon the slope of the emerald turf its crystal dominion began. My position enabled me to include in a single view both the eastern and western extremities of the islet, and I observed a singularly-marked difference in their aspects. The latter was all one radiant harem of garden beauties. It glowed and blushed beneath the eye of the slant sunlight, and fairly laughed with flowers. The grass was short, springy, sweet-scented, and Asphodel-interspersed. The trees were lithe, mirthful, erect, bright, slender, and graceful, of eastern figure and foliage, with bark smooth, glossy, and parti-colored. There seemed a deep sense of life and joy about all, and although no airs blew from out the heavens, yet everything had motion through the gentle sweepings to and fro of innumerable butterflies, that might have been mistaken for tulips with wings [4].

The other or eastern end of the isle was whelmed in the blackest shade. A sombre, yet beautiful and peaceful gloom, here pervaded all things. The trees were dark in color and mournful in form and attitude-- wreathing themselves into sad, solemn, and spectral shapes, that conveyed ideas of mortal sorrow and untimely death. The grass wore the deep tint of the cypress, and the heads of its blades hung droopingly, and hither and thither among it were many small unsightly hillocks, low and narrow, and not very long, that had the aspect of graves, but were not, although over and all about them the rue and the rosemary clambered. The shades of the trees fell heavily upon the water, and seemed to bury itself therein, impregnating the depths of the element with darkness. I fancied that each shadow, as the sun descended lower and lower, separated itself sullenly from the trunk that gave it birth, and thus became absorbed by the stream, while other shadows issued momently from the trees, taking the place of their predecessors thus entombed.

This idea having once seized upon my fancy greatly excited it, and I lost myself forthwith in reverie. "If ever island were enchanted," said I to myself, "this is it. This is the haunt of the few gentle Fays who remain from the wreck of the race. Are these green tombs theirs?--or do they yield up their sweet lives as mankind yield up their own? In dying, do they not rather waste away mournfully, rendering unto God little by little their existence, as these trees render up shadow after shadow, exhausting their substance unto dissolution? What the wasting tree is to the water that imbibes its shade, growing thus blacker by what it preys upon, may not the life of the Fay be to the death which engulfs it?"

As I thus mused, with half-shut eyes, while the sun sank rapidly to rest, and eddying currents careered round and round the island, bearing upon their bosom large dazzling white flakes of the bark of the sycamore, flakes which, in their multiform positions upon the water, a quick imagination might have converted into anything it pleased; while I thus mused, it appeared to me that the form of one of those very Fays about whom I had been pondering, made its way slowly into the darkness from out the light at the western end of the island. She stood erect in a singularly fragile canoe, and urged it with the mere phantom of an oar. While within the influence of the lingering sunbeams, her attitude seemed indicative of joy, but sorrow deformed it as she passed within the shade. Slowly she glided along, and at length rounded the islet and re-entered the region of light. "The revolution which has just been made by the Fay," continued I musingly, "is the cycle of the brief year of her life. She has floated through her winter and through her summer. She is a year nearer unto death: for I did not fail to see that as she came into the shade, her shadow fell from her, and was swallowed up in the dark water, making its blackness more black."

And again the boat appeared and the Fay, but about the attitude of the latter there was more of care and uncertainty and less of elastic joy. She floated again from out the light and into the gloom (which deepened momently), and again her shadow fell from her into the ebony water, and became absorbed into its blackness. And again and again she made the circuit of the island (while the sun rushed down to his slumbers), and at each issuing into the light there was more sorrow about her person, while it grew feebler and far fainter and more indistinct, and at each passage into the gloom there fell from her a darker shade, which became whelmed in a shadow more black. But at length, when the sun had utterly departed, the Fay, now the mere ghost of her former self, went disconsolately with her boat into the region of the ebony flood, and that she issued thence at all I cannot say, for darkness fell over all things, and I beheld her magical figure no more.

Footnotes:

1. Moraux is here derived from moeurs, and its meaning is "fashionable," or, more strictly, "of manners."

2. Speaking of the tides, Pomponius Mela, in his treatise, 'De Sitû Orbis', says,

"Either the world is a great animal, or," etc.

3. Balzac, in substance; I do not remember the words.

4. "Florem putares nare per liquidum æthera."

'P. Commire'.

THE POWER OF WORDS

'Oinos.'
   Pardon, Agathos, the weakness of a spirit new-fledged with immortality!

'Agathos.'
   You have spoken nothing, my Oinos, for which pardon is to be demanded. Not even here is knowledge a thing of intuition. For wisdom, ask of the angels freely, that it may be given!

'Oinos.'
   But in this existence I dreamed that I should be at once cognizant of all things, and thus at once happy in being cognizant of all.

'Agathos.'
   Ah, not in knowledge is happiness, but in the acquisition of knowledge! In forever knowing, we are forever blessed; but to know all, were the curse of a fiend.

'Oinos.'
   But does not The Most High know all?

'Agathos'.
   That (since he is The Most Happy) must be still the one thing unknown even to HIM.

'Oinos.'
   But, since we grow hourly in knowledge, must not at last all things be known?

'Agathos.'
   Look down into the abysmal distances!--attempt to force the gaze down the multitudinous vistas of the stars, as we sweep slowly through them thus--and thus--and thus! Even the spiritual vision, is it not at all points arrested by the continuous golden walls of the universe?—the walls of the myriads of the shining bodies that mere number has appeared to blend into unity?

'Oinos'.
   I clearly perceive that the infinity of matter is no dream.

'Agathos'.
   There are no dreams in Aidenn--but it is here whispered that, of this infinity of matter, the sole purpose is to afford infinite springs at which the soul may allay the thirst to know which is forever unquenchable within it--since to

quench it would be to extinguish the soul's self. Question me then, my Oinos, freely and without fear. Come! we will leave to the left the loud harmony of the Pleiades, and swoop outward from the throne into the starry meadows beyond Orion, where, for pansies and violets, and heart's-ease, are the beds of the triplicate and triple-tinted suns.

'Oinos'.
And now, Agathos, as we proceed, instruct me!--speak to me in the earth's familiar tones! I understand not what you hinted to me just now of the modes or of the methods of what during mortality, we were accustomed to call Creation. Do you mean to say that the Creator is not God?

'Agathos'.
I mean to say that the Deity does not create.

'Oinos'.
Explain!

'Agathos'.
In the beginning only, he created. The seeming creatures which are now throughout the universe so perpetually springing into being can only be considered as the mediate or indirect, not as the direct or immediate results of the Divine creative power.

'Oinos.'
Among men, my Agathos, this idea would be considered heretical in the extreme.

'Agathos.'
Among the angels, my Oinos, it is seen to be simply true.

'Oinos.'
I can comprehend you thus far--that certain operations of what we term Nature, or the natural laws, will, under certain conditions, give rise to that which has all the appearance of creation. Shortly before the final overthrow of the earth, there were, I well remember, many very successful experiments in what some philosophers were weak enough to denominate the creation of animalculæ.

'Agathos.'
The cases of which you speak were, in fact, instances of the secondary creation, and of the only species of creation which has ever been since the first word spoke into existence the first law.

'Oinos.'
Are not the starry worlds that, from the abyss of nonentity, burst hourly forth into the heavens--are not these stars, Agathos, the immediate handiwork of the King?

'Agathos.'

Let me endeavor, my Oinos, to lead you, step by step, to the conception I intend. You are well aware that, as no thought can perish, so no act is without infinite result. We moved our hands, for example, when we were dwellers on the earth, and in so doing we gave vibration to the atmosphere which engirdled it. This vibration was indefinitely extended till it gave impulse to every particle of the earth's air, which thenceforward, and forever, was actuated by the one movement of the hand. This fact the mathematicians of our globe well knew. They made the special effects, indeed, wrought in the fluid by special impulses, the subject of exact calculation--so that it became easy to determine in what precise period an impulse of given extent would engirdle the orb, and impress (forever) every atom of the atmosphere circumambient. Retrograding, they found no difficulty; from a given effect, under given conditions, in determining the value of the original impulse. Now the mathematicians who saw that the results of any given impulse were absolutely endless--and who saw that a portion of these results were accurately traceable through the agency of algebraic analysis--who saw, too, the facility of the retrogradation--these men saw, at the same time, that this species of analysis itself had within itself a capacity for indefinite progress--that there were no bounds conceivable to its advancement and applicability, except within the intellect of him who advanced or applied it. But at this point our mathematicians paused.

'Oinos.'

And why, Agathos, should they have proceeded?

'Agathos.'

Because there were some considerations of deep interest beyond. It was deducible from what they knew, that to a being of infinite understanding--one to whom the perfection of the algebraic analysis lay unfolded--there could be no difficulty in tracing every impulse given the air--and the ether through the air--to the remotest consequences at any even infinitely remote epoch of time. It is indeed demonstrable that every such impulse given the air, must in the end impress every individual thing that exists within the universe;--and the being of infinite understanding--the being whom we have imagined--might trace the remote undulations of the impulse--trace them upward and onward in their influences upon all particles of all matter--upward and onward forever in their modifications of old forms--or, in other words, in their creation of new--until he found them reflected--unimpressive at last--back from the throne of the Godhead. And not only could such a being do this, but at any epoch, should a given result be afforded him--should one of these numberless comets, for example, be presented to his inspection--he could have no difficulty in determining, by the analytic retrogradation, to what original impulse it was due. This power of retrogradation in its absolute fulness and perfection—this faculty of referring at all epochs, all effects to all causes--is of course the prerogative of the Deity alone--but in every variety of degree, short of the absolute perfection, is the power itself exercised by the whole host of the Angelic Intelligences.

'Oinos'.

But you speak merely of impulses upon the air.

'Agathos'.

In speaking of the air, I referred only to the earth: but the general proposition has reference to impulses upon the ether--which, since it pervades, and alone pervades all space, is thus the great medium of creation.

'Oinos'.

Then all motion, of whatever nature, creates?

'Agathos'.

It must: but a true philosophy has long taught that the source of all motion is thought--and the source of all thought is--

'Oinos'.

God.

'Agathos'.

I have spoken to you, Oinos, as to a child, of the fair Earth which lately perished--of impulses upon the atmosphere of the earth.

'Oinos'.

You did.

'Agathos'.

And while I thus spoke, did there not cross your mind some thought of the physical power of words? Is not every word an impulse on the air?

'Oinos'.

But why, Agathos, do you weep--and why, oh, why do your wings droop as we hover above this fair star--which is the greenest and yet most terrible of all we have encountered in our flight? Its brilliant flowers look like a fairy dream--but its fierce volcanoes like the passions of a turbulent heart.

'Agathos'.

They are!--they are!--This wild star--it is now three centuries since, with clasped hands, and with streaming eyes, at the feet of my beloved--I spoke it-- with a few passionate sentences--into birth. Its brilliant flowers are the dearest of all unfulfilled dreams, and its raging volcanoes are the passions of the most turbulent and unhallowed of hearts!

THE COLLOQUY OF MONOS AND UNA

[Greek: Mellontasauta']

These things are in the future.
    Sophocles--'Antig.'

'Una.'
    "Born again?"

'Monos.'
    Yes, fairest and best beloved Una, "born again." These were the words upon whose mystical meaning I had so long pondered, rejecting the explanations of the priesthood, until Death itself resolved for me the secret.

'Una.'
    Death!

'Monos.'
    How strangely, sweet Una, you echo my words! I observe, too, a vacillation in your step, a joyous inquietude in your eyes. You are confused and oppressed by the majestic novelty of the Life Eternal. Yes, it was of Death I spoke. And here how singularly sounds that word which of old was wont to bring terror to all hearts, throwing a mildew upon all pleasures!

'Una.'
    Ah, Death, the spectre which sate at all feasts! How often, Monos, did we lose ourselves in speculations upon its nature! How mysteriously did it act as a check to human bliss, saying unto it, "thus far, and no farther!" That earnest mutual love, my own Monos, which burned within our bosoms, how vainly did we flatter ourselves, feeling happy in its first upspringing that our happiness would strengthen with its strength! Alas, as it grew, so grew in our hearts the dread of that evil hour which was hurrying to separate us forever! Thus in time it became painful to love. Hate would have been mercy then.

'Monos'.
    Speak not here of these griefs, dear Una--mine, mine forever now!

'Una'.
    But the memory of past sorrow, is it not present joy? I have much to say yet of the things which have been. Above all, I burn to know the incidents of your own passage through the dark Valley and Shadow.

'Monos'.

And when did the radiant Una ask anything of her Monos in vain? I will be minute in relating all, but at what point shall the weird narrative begin?

'Una'.

At what point?

'Monos'.

You have said.

'Una'.

Monos, I comprehend you. In Death we have both learned the propensity of man to define the indefinable. I will not say, then, commence with the moment of life's cessation--but commence with that sad, sad instant when, the fever having abandoned you, you sank into a breathless and motionless torpor, and I pressed down your pallid eyelids with the passionate fingers of love.

'Monos'.

One word first, my Una, in regard to man's general condition at this epoch. You will remember that one or two of the wise among our forefathers--wise in fact, although not in the world's esteem--had ventured to doubt the propriety of the term "improvement," as applied to the progress of our civilization. There were periods in each of the five or six centuries immediately preceding our dissolution when arose some vigorous intellect, boldly contending for those principles whose truth appears now, to our disenfranchised reason, so utterly obvious --principles which should have taught our race to submit to the guidance of the natural laws rather than attempt their control. At long intervals some master-minds appeared, looking upon each advance in practical science as a retrogradation in the true utility. Occasionally the poetic intellect--that intellect which we now feel to have been the most exalted of all--since those truths which to us were of the most enduring importance could only be reached by that analogy which speaks in proof-tones to the imagination alone, and to the unaided reason bears no weight--occasionally did this poetic intellect proceed a step farther in the evolving of the vague idea of the philosophic, and find in the mystic parable that tells of the tree of knowledge, and of its forbidden fruit, death-producing, a distinct intimation that knowledge was not meet for man in the infant condition of his soul. And these men--the poets--living and perishing amid the scorn of the "utilitarians"--of rough pedants, who arrogated to themselves a title which could have been properly applied only to the scorned--these men, the poets, pondered piningly, yet not unwisely, upon the ancient days when our wants were not more simple than our enjoyments were keen--days when mirth was a word unknown, so solemnly deep-toned was happiness--holy, august, and blissful days, blue rivers ran undammed, between hills unhewn, into far forest solitudes, primeval, odorous, and unexplored. Yet these noble exceptions from the general misrule served but to strengthen it by opposition. Alas! we had fallen upon the most evil of all our evil days. The great "movement"--that was the cant term--went on: a diseased commotion, moral and physical. Art--the Arts--arose supreme, and once enthroned, cast chains upon the intellect which had elevated them to power. Man, because he could not but acknowledge the majesty of Nature, fell into childish exultation at his acquired and still-increasing dominion over her elements. Even while he stalked a God in his own fancy, an infantine imbecility came over him. As might be supposed from the origin of his disorder, he grew infected with system, and with abstraction. He enwrapped himself in generalities. Among other odd ideas, that of universal equality gained ground; and in the face of analogy and of God--in despite of the loud warning voice of the laws of gradation so visibly pervading all things in Earth and Heaven--wild attempts at an omniprevalent Democracy were made. Yet this evil sprang necessarily from the leading evil, Knowledge. Man could not both know and succumb. Meantime huge smoking cities arose, innumerable. Green leaves shrank before the hot breath of furnaces. The fair face of Nature was deformed as with the ravages of some loathsome disease. And methinks, sweet Una, even our slumbering sense of the forced and of the far-fetched might have arrested us here. But now it appears that we had worked out our own destruction in the perversion of our taste, or rather in the blind neglect of its culture in the schools. For, in truth, it was at this crisis that taste alone--that faculty which, holding a middle position between the pure intellect and the moral sense, could never safely have been disregarded--it was now that taste alone could have led us gently back to Beauty, to Nature, and to Life. But alas for the pure contemplative spirit and majestic intuition of Plato! Alas for the [Greek: mousichae]which he justly regarded as an all-sufficient education for the soul! Alas for him and for it!--since both were most desperately needed, when both were most entirely forgotten or despised[1]. Pascal, a philosopher whom we both love, has said, how truly!--"Que tout notre raisonnement se réduit à céder au sentiment;" and it is not impossible that the sentiment of the natural, had time permitted it, would have regained its old ascendency over the harsh mathematical reason of the schools. But this thing was not to be. Prematurely induced by intemperance of knowledge, the old age of the world drew near. This the mass of mankind saw not, or, living lustily although unhappily, affected not to see. But, for myself, the Earth's records had taught me to look for widest ruin as the price of highest civilization. I had imbibed a prescience of our Fate from comparison of China the simple and enduring, with Assyria the architect, with Egypt the astrologer, with Nubia, more crafty than either, the turbulent mother of all Arts. In the history of these regions I met with a ray from the Future. The individual artificialities of the three latter were local diseases of the Earth, and in their individual overthrows we had seen local remedies applied; but for the infected world at large I could anticipate no regeneration save in death. That man, as a race, should not become extinct, I saw that he must be "born again."

And now it was, fairest and dearest, that we wrapped our spirits, daily, in dreams. Now it was that, in twilight, we discoursed of the days to come, when the Art-scarred surface of the Earth, having undergone that purification which alone could efface its rectangular obscenities, should clothe itself anew in the verdure and the mountain-slopes and the smiling waters of Paradise, and be rendered at length a fit dwelling-place for man:--for man the Death-purged--for man to whose now exalted intellect there should be poison in knowledge no more--for the redeemed, regenerated, blissful, and now immortal, but still for the material, man.

'Una'.

Well do I remember these conversations, dear Monos; but the epoch of the fiery overthrow was not so near at hand as we believed, and as the corruption you indicate did surely warrant us in believing. Men lived; and died individually. You yourself sickened, and passed into the grave; and thither your constant Una speedily followed you. And though the century which has since elapsed, and whose conclusion brings up together once more, tortured our slumbering senses with no impatience of duration, yet my Monos, it was a century still.

'Monos'.

Say, rather, a point in the vague infinity. Unquestionably, it was in the Earth's dotage that I died. Wearied at heart with anxieties which had their origin in the general turmoil and decay, I succumbed to the fierce fever. After some few days of pain, and many of dreamy delirium replete with ecstasy, the manifestations of which you mistook for pain, while I longed but was impotent to undeceive you--after some days there came upon me, as you have said, a breathless and motionless torpor; and this was termed Death by those who stood around me.

Words are vague things. My condition did not deprive me of sentience. It appeared to me not greatly dissimilar to the extreme quiescence of him, who, having slumbered long and profoundly, lying motionless and fully prostrate in a mid-summer noon, begins to steal slowly back into consciousness, through the mere sufficiency of his sleep, and without being awakened by external disturbances.

I breathed no longer. The pulses were still. The heart had ceased to beat. Volition had not departed, but was powerless. The senses were unusually active, although eccentrically so--assuming often each other's functions at random. The taste and the smell were inextricably confounded, and became one sentiment, abnormal and intense. The rose-water with which your tenderness had moistened my lips to the last, affected me with sweet fancies of flowers-- fantastic flowers, far more lovely than any of the old Earth, but whose prototypes we have here blooming around us. The eye-lids, transparent and bloodless, offered no complete impediment to vision. As volition was in abeyance, the balls could not roll in their sockets--but all objects within the range of the visual hemisphere were seen with more or less distinctness; the rays which fell upon the external retina, or into the corner of the eye, producing a more vivid effect than those which struck the front or interior surface. Yet, in the former instance, this effect was so far anomalous that I appreciated it only as sound--sound sweet or discordant as the matters presenting themselves at my side were light or dark in shade--curved or angular in outline. The hearing, at the same time, although excited in degree, was not irregular in action-- estimating real sounds with an extravagance of precision, not less than of sensibility. Touch had undergone a modification more peculiar. Its impressions were tardily received, but pertinaciously retained, and resulted always in the highest physical pleasure. Thus the pressure of your sweet fingers upon my eyelids, at first only recognized through vision, at length, long after their removal, filled my whole being with a sensual delight immeasurable. I say with a sensual delight. All my perceptions were purely sensual. The materials furnished the passive brain by the senses were not in the least degree wrought into shape by the deceased understanding. Of pain there was some little; of pleasure there was much; but of moral pain or pleasure none at all. Thus your wild sobs floated into my ear with all their mournful cadences, and were appreciated in their every variation of sad tone; but they were soft musical sounds and no more; they conveyed to the extinct reason no intimation of the sorrows which gave them birth; while large and constant tears which fell upon my face, telling the bystanders of a heart which broke, thrilled every fibre of my frame with ecstasy alone. And this was in truth the Death of which these bystanders spoke reverently, in low whispers--you, sweet Una, gaspingly, with loud cries.

They attired me for the coffin--three or four dark figures which flitted busily to and fro. As these crossed the direct line of my vision they affected me as forms; but upon passing to my side their images impressed me with the idea of shrieks, groans, and, other dismal expressions of terror, of horror, or of woe. You alone, habited in a white robe, passed in all directions musically about.

The day waned; and, as its light faded away, I became possessed by a vague uneasiness--an anxiety such as the sleeper feels when sad real sounds fall continuously within his ear--low distant bell-tones, solemn, at long but equal intervals, and commingling with melancholy dreams. Night arrived; and with its shadows a heavy discomfort. It oppressed my limbs with the oppression of some dull weight, and was palpable. There was also a moaning sound, not unlike the distant reverberation of surf, but more continuous, which, beginning with the first twilight, had grown in strength with the darkness. Suddenly lights were brought into the rooms, and this reverberation became forthwith interrupted into frequent unequal bursts of the same sound, but less dreary and less distinct. The ponderous oppression was in a great measure relieved; and, issuing from the flame of each lamp (for there were many), there flowed unbrokenly into my ears a strain of melodious monotone. And when now, dear Una, approaching the bed upon which I lay outstretched, you sat gently by my side, breathing odor from your sweet lips, and pressing them upon my brow, there arose tremulously within my bosom, and mingling with the merely physical sensations which circumstances had called forth, a something akin to sentiment itself--a feeling that, half appreciating, half responded to your earnest love and sorrow; but this feeling took no root in the pulseless heart, and seemed indeed rather a shadow than a reality, and faded quickly away, first into extreme quiescence, and then into a purely sensual pleasure as before.

And now, from the wreck and the chaos of the usual senses, there appeared to have arisen within me a sixth, all perfect. In its exercise I found a wild delight--yet a delight still physical, inasmuch as the understanding had in it no part. Motion in the animal frame had fully ceased. No muscle quivered; no nerve thrilled; no artery throbbed. But there seemed to have sprung up in the brain that of which no words could convey to the merely human intelligence even an indistinct conception. Let me term it a mental pendulous pulsation. It was the moral embodiment of man's abstract idea of Time. By the absolute equalization of this movement--or of such as this--had the cycles of the firmamental orbs themselves been adjusted. By its aid I measured the irregularities of the clock upon the mantel, and of the watches of the attendants. Their tickings came sonorously to my ears. The slightest deviations from the true proportion--and these deviations were omniprevalent--affected me just as violations of abstract truth were wont on earth to affect the moral sense.

Although no two of the timepieces in the chamber struck the individual seconds accurately together, yet I had no difficulty in holding steadily in mind the tones, and the respective momentary errors of each. And this--this keen, perfect self-existing sentiment of duration--this sentiment existing (as man could not possibly have conceived it to exist) independently of any succession of events--this idea--this sixth sense, upspringing from the ashes of the rest, was the first obvious and certain step of the intemporal soul upon the threshold of the temporal eternity.

It was midnight; and you still sat by my side. All others had departed from the chamber of Death. They had deposited me in the coffin. The lamps burned flickeringly; for this I knew by the tremulousness of the monotonous strains. But suddenly these strains diminished in distinctness and in volume. Finally they ceased. The perfume in my nostrils died away. Forms affected my vision no longer. The oppression of the Darkness uplifted itself from my bosom. A dull shot like that of electricity pervaded my frame, and was followed by total loss of the idea of contact. All of what man has termed sense was merged in the sole consciousness of entity, and in the one abiding sentiment of duration. The mortal body had been at length stricken with the hand of the deadly Decay.

Yet had not all of sentience departed; for the consciousness and the sentiment remaining supplied some of its functions by a lethargic intuition. I appreciated the direful change now in operation upon the flesh, and, as the dreamer is sometimes aware of the bodily presence of one who leans over him, so, sweet Una, I still dully felt that you sat by my side. So, too, when the noon of the second day came, I was not unconscious of those movements which displaced you from my side, which confined me within the coffin, which deposited me within the hearse, which bore me to the grave, which lowered me within it, which heaped heavily the mould upon me, and which thus left me, in blackness and corruption, to my sad and solemn slumbers with the worm.

And here in the prison-house which has few secrets to disclose, there rolled away days and weeks and months; and the soul watched narrowly each second as it flew, and, without effort, took record of its flight--without effort and without object.

A year passed. The consciousness of being had grown hourly more indistinct, and that of mere locality had in great measure usurped its position. The idea of entity was becoming merged in that of place. The narrow space immediately surrounding what had been the body was now growing to be the body itself. At length, as often happens to the sleeper (by sleep and its world alone is Death imaged)--at length, as sometimes happened on Earth to the deep slumberer, when some flitting light half startled him into awaking, yet left him half enveloped in dreams--so to me, in the strict embrace of the Shadow, came that light which alone might have had power to startle--the light of enduring Love. Men toiled at the grave in which I lay darkling. They upthrew the damp earth. Upon my mouldering bones there descended the coffin of Una. And now again all was void. That nebulous light had been extinguished. That feeble thrill had vibrated itself into quiescence. Many lustra had supervened. Dust had returned to dust. The worm had food no more. The sense of being had at length utterly departed, and there reigned in its stead--instead of all things, dominant and perpetual--the autocrats Place and Time. For that which was not--for that which had no form--for that which had no thought--for that which had no sentience--for that which was soundless, yet of which matter formed no portion--for all this nothingness, yet for all this immortality, the grave was still a home, and the corrosive hours, co-mates.

Footnotes:

1. "It will be hard to discover a better [method of education] than that which the experience of so many ages has already discovered; and this may be summed up as consisting in gymnastics for the body, and music for the soul."

Repub. lib. 2.

"For this reason is a musical education most essential; since it causes Rhythm and Harmony to penetrate most intimately into the soul, taking the strongest hold upon it, filling it with beauty and making the man beautiful-minded. ... He will praise and admire the beautiful, will receive it with joy into his soul, will feed upon it, and assimilate his own condition with it."

Ibid. lib. 3. Music had, however, among the Athenians, a far more comprehensive signification than with us. It included not only the harmonies of time and of tune, but the poetic diction, sentiment and creation, each in its widest sense. The study of music was with them, in fact, the general cultivation of the taste--of that which recognizes the beautiful--in contradistinction from reason, which deals only with the true.

THE CONVERSATION OF EIROS AND CHARMION

I will bring fire to thee.
    Euripides.--'Androm'.

'Eiros'.
    Why do you call me Eiros?

'Charmion'.
    So henceforward will you always be called. You must forget, too, my earthly name, and speak to me as Charmion.

'Eiros'.
    This is indeed no dream!

'Charmion'.
    Dreams are with us no more;--but of these mysteries anon. I rejoice to see you looking life-like and rational. The film of the shadow has already passed from off your eyes. Be of heart, and fear nothing. Your allotted days of stupor have expired, and to-morrow I will myself induct you into the full joys and wonders of your novel existence.

'Eiros'.
    True--I feel no stupor--none at all. The wild sickness and the terrible darkness have left me, and I hear no longer that mad, rushing, horrible sound, like the "voice of many waters." Yet my senses are bewildered, Charmion, with the keenness of their perception of the new.

'Charmion'.
    A few days will remove all this;--but I fully understand you, and feel for you. It is now ten earthly years since I underwent what you undergo--yet the remembrance of it hangs by me still. You have now suffered all of pain, however, which you will suffer in Aidenn.

'Eiros'.
    In Aidenn?

'Charmion'.
    In Aidenn.

'Eiros'.
    O God!--pity me, Charmion!--I am overburthened with the majesty of all things--of the unknown now known--of the speculative Future merged in the august and certain Present.

'Charmion'.
   Grapple not now with such thoughts. To-morrow we will speak of this. Your mind wavers, and its agitation will find relief in the exercise of simple memories. Look not around, nor forward--but back. I am burning with anxiety to hear the details of that stupendous event which threw you among us. Tell me of it. Let us converse of familiar things, in the old familiar language of the world which has so fearfully perished.

'Eiros'.
   Most fearfully, fearfully!--this is indeed no dream.

'Charmion'.
   Dreams are no more. Was I much mourned, my Eiros?

'Eiros'.
   Mourned, Charmion?--oh, deeply. To that last hour of all there hung a cloud of intense gloom and devout sorrow over your household.

'Charmion'.
   And that last hour--speak of it. Remember that, beyond the naked fact of the catastrophe itself, I know nothing. When, coming out from among mankind, I passed into Night through the Grave--at that period, if I remember aright, the calamity which overwhelmed you was utterly unanticipated. But, indeed, I knew little of the speculative philosophy of the day.

'Eiros'.
   The individual calamity was, as you say, entirely unanticipated; but analogous misfortunes had been long a subject of discussion with astronomers. I need scarce tell you, my friend, that, even when you left us, men had agreed to understand those passages in the most holy writings which speak of the final destruction of all things by fire as having reference to the orb of the earth alone, But in regard to the immediate agency of the ruin, speculation had been at fault from that epoch in astronomical knowledge in which the comets were divested of the terrors of flame. The very moderate density of these bodies had been well established. They had been observed to pass among the satellites of Jupiter without bringing about any sensible alteration either in the masses or in the orbits of these secondary planets. We had long regarded the wanderers as vapory creations of inconceivable tenuity, and as altogether incapable of doing injury to our substantial globe, even in the event of contact. But contact was not in any degree dreaded; for the elements of all the comets were accurately known. That among them we should look for the agency of the threatened fiery destruction had been for many years considered an inadmissible idea. But wonders and wild fancies had been of late days strangely rife among mankind; and, although it was only with a few of the ignorant that actual apprehension prevailed, upon the announcement by astronomers of a new comet, yet this announcement was generally received with I know not what of agitation and mistrust.
   The elements of the strange orb were immediately calculated, and it was at once conceded by all observers that its path, at perihelion would bring it into very close proximity with the earth. There were two or three astronomers of

secondary note who resolutely maintained that a contact was inevitable. I cannot very well express to you the effect of this intelligence upon the people. For a few short days they would not believe an assertion which their intellect, so long employed among worldly considerations, could not in any manner grasp. But the truth of a vitally important fact soon makes its way into the understanding of even the most stolid. Finally, all men saw that astronomical knowledge lies not, and they awaited the comet. Its approach was not at first seemingly rapid, nor was its appearance of very unusual character. It was of a dull red, and had little perceptible train. For seven or eight days we saw no material increase in its apparent diameter, and but a partial alteration in its color. Meantime, the ordinary affairs of men were discarded, and all interest absorbed in a growing discussion instituted by the philosophic in respect to the cometary nature. Even the grossly ignorant aroused their sluggish capacities to such considerations. The learned now gave their intellect--their soul--to no such points as the allaying of fear, or to the sustenance of loved theory. They sought--they panted for right views. They groaned for perfected knowledge. Truth arose in the purity of her strength and exceeding majesty, and the wise bowed down and adored.

That material injury to our globe or to its inhabitants would result from the apprehended contact was an opinion which hourly lost ground among the wise; and the wise were now freely permitted to rule the reason and the fancy of the crowd. It was demonstrated that the density of the comet's nucleus was far less than that of our rarest gas; and the harmless passage of a similar visitor among the satellites of Jupiter was a point strongly insisted upon, and which served greatly to allay terror. Theologists, with an earnestness fear-enkindled, dwelt upon the biblical prophecies, and expounded them to the people with a directness and simplicity of which no previous instance had been known. That the final destruction of the earth must be brought about by the agency of fire, was urged with a spirit that enforced everywhere conviction; and that the comets were of no fiery nature (as all men now knew) was a truth which relieved all, in a great measure, from the apprehension of the great calamity foretold. It is noticeable that the popular prejudices and vulgar errors in regard to pestilences and wars--errors which were wont to prevail upon every appearance of a comet--were now altogether unknown, as if by some sudden convulsive exertion reason had at once hurled superstition from her throne. The feeblest intellect had derived vigor from excessive interest.

What minor evils might arise from the contact were points of elaborate question. The learned spoke of slight geological disturbances, of probable alterations in climate, and consequently in vegetation; of possible magnetic and electric influences. Many held that no visible or perceptible effect would in any manner be produced. While such discussions were going on, their subject gradually approached, growing larger in apparent diameter, and of a more brilliant lustre. Mankind grew paler as it came. All human operations were suspended.

There was an epoch in the course of the general sentiment when the comet had attained, at length, a size surpassing that of any previously recorded visitation. The people now, dismissing any lingering hope that the astronomers were wrong, experienced all the certainty of evil. The chimerical aspect of their terror was gone. The hearts of the stoutest of our race beat violently within their bosoms. A very few days suffered, however, to merge even such feelings in sentiments more unendurable. We could no longer apply to the strange orb any accustomed thoughts. Its historical attributes had disappeared. It oppressed us with a hideous novelty of emotion. We saw it not as an astronomical phenomenon in the heavens, but as an incubus upon our hearts and a shadow upon our brains. It had taken, with unconceivable rapidity, the character of a gigantic mantle of rare flame, extending from horizon to horizon.

Yet a day, and men breathed with greater freedom. It was clear that we were already within the influence of the comet; yet we lived. We even felt an unusual elasticity of frame and vivacity of mind. The exceeding tenuity of the object of our dread was apparent; for all heavenly objects were plainly visible through it. Meantime, our vegetation had perceptibly altered; and we gained faith, from this predicted circumstance, in the foresight of the wise. A wild luxuriance of foliage, utterly unknown before, burst out upon every vegetable thing.

Yet another day--and the evil was not altogether upon us. It was now evident that its nucleus would first reach us. A wild change had come over all men; and the first sense of pain was the wild signal for general lamentation and horror. The first sense of pain lay in a rigorous construction of the breast and lungs, and an insufferable dryness of the skin. It could not be denied that our atmosphere was radically affected; the conformation of this atmosphere and the possible modifications to which it might be subjected, were now the topics of discussion. The result of investigation sent an electric thrill of the intensest terror through the universal heart of man.

It had been long known that the air which encircled us was a compound of oxygen and nitrogen gases, in the proportion of twenty-one measures of oxygen and seventy-nine of nitrogen in every one hundred of the atmosphere. Oxygen, which was the principle of combustion, and the vehicle of heat, was absolutely necessary to the support of animal life, and was the most powerful and energetic agent in nature. Nitrogen, on the contrary, was incapable of supporting either animal life or flame. An unnatural excess of oxygen would result, it had been ascertained, in just such an elevation of the animal spirits as we had latterly experienced. It was the pursuit, the extension of the idea, which had engendered awe. What would be the result of a total extraction of the nitrogen? A combustion irresistible, all-devouring, omni-prevalent, immediate;--the entire fulfilment, in all their minute and terrible details, of the fiery and horror-inspiring denunciations of the prophecies of the Holy Book.

Why need I paint, Charmion, the now disenchained frenzy of mankind? That tenuity in the comet which had previously inspired us with hope, was now the source of the bitterness of despair. In its impalpable gaseous character we clearly perceived the consummation of Fate. Meantime a day again passed--bearing away with it the last shadow of Hope. We gasped in the rapid modification of the air. The red blood bounded tumultuously through its strict channels. A furious delirium possessed all men; and with arms rigidly outstretched towards the threatening heavens, they trembled and shrieked aloud. But the nucleus of the destroyer was now upon us;--even here in Aidenn I shudder while I speak. Let me be brief--brief as the ruin that overwhelmed. For a moment there was a wild lurid light alone, visiting and penetrating all things. Then--let us bow down, Charmion, before the excessive majesty of the great God!--then, there came a shouting and pervading sound, as if from the mouth itself of HIM; while the whole incumbent mass of ether in which we existed, burst at once into a species of intense flame, for whose surpassing brilliancy and all-fervid heat even the angels in the high Heaven of pure knowledge have no name. Thus ended all.

SHADOW---A PARABLE

Yea! though I walk through the valley of the Shadow.
   'Psalm of David'.

Ye who read are still among the living; but I who write shall have long since gone my way into the region of shadows. For indeed strange things shall happen, and secret things be known, and many centuries shall pass away, ere these memorials be seen of men. And, when seen, there will be some to disbelieve and some to doubt, and yet a few who will find much to ponder upon in the characters here graven with a stylus of iron.

The year had been a year of terror, and of feeling more intense than terror for which there is no name upon the earth. For many prodigies and signs had taken place, and far and wide, over sea and land, the black wings of the Pestilence were spread abroad. To those, nevertheless, cunning in the stars, it was not unknown that the heavens wore an aspect of ill; and to me, the Greek Oinos, among others, it was evident that now had arrived the alternation of that seven hundred and ninety-fourth year when, at the entrance of Aries, the planet Jupiter is enjoined with the red ring of the terrible Saturnus. The peculiar spirit of the skies, if I mistake not greatly, made itself manifest, not only in the physical orb of the earth, but in the souls, imaginations, and meditations of mankind.

Over some flasks of the red Chian wine, within the walls of a noble hall, in a dim city called Ptolemais, we sat, at night, a company of seven. And to our chamber there was no entrance save by a lofty door of brass: and the door was fashioned by the artisan Corinnos, and, being of rare workmanship, was fastened from within. Black draperies, likewise in the gloomy room, shut out from our view the moon, the lurid stars, and the peopleless streets--but the boding and the memory of Evil, they would not be so excluded. There were things around us and about of which I can render no distinct account--things material and spiritual-- heaviness in the atmosphere--a sense of suffocation-- anxiety--and, above all, that terrible state of existence which the nervous experience when the senses are keenly living and awake, and meanwhile the powers of thought lie dormant. A dead weight hung upon us. It hung upon our limbs--upon the household furniture--upon the goblets from which we drank; and all things were depressed, and borne down thereby--all things save only the flames of the seven iron lamps which illumined our revel. Uprearing themselves in tall slender lines of light, they thus remained burning all pallid and motionless; and in the mirror which their lustre formed upon the round table of ebony at which we sat each of us there assembled beheld the pallor of his own countenance, and the unquiet glare in the downcast eyes of his companions. Yet we laughed and were merry in our proper way--which was hysterical; and sang the songs of Anacreon--which are madness; and drank deeply--although the purple wine reminded us of blood. For there was yet another tenant of our chamber in the person of young Zoilus. Dead and at full length he lay, enshrouded;--the genius and the demon of the scene. Alas! he bore no portion in our mirth, save that his countenance, distorted with the plague, and his eyes in which Death had but half extinguished the fire of the pestilence, seemed to take such an interest in our merriment as the dead may haply take in the merriment of those who are to die. But although I, Oinos, felt that the eyes of the departed were upon me, still I forced myself not to perceive the bitterness of their expression, and gazing down steadily into the depths of the ebony mirror, sang with a loud and sonorous voice the songs of the son of Teos. But gradually my songs they ceased, and their echoes, rolling afar off among the sable draperies of the chamber, became weak, and undistinguishable, and so faded away. And lo! from among those sable draperies, where the sounds of the song departed, there came forth a dark and undefiled shadow--a shadow such as the moon, when low in heaven, might fashion from the figure of a man: but it was the shadow neither of man nor of God, nor of any familiar thing. And quivering awhile among the draperies of the room it at length rested in full view upon the surface of the door of brass. But the shadow was vague, and formless, and indefinite, and was the shadow neither of man nor God--neither God of Greece, nor God of Chaldæa, nor any Egyptian God. And the shadow rested upon the brazen doorway, and under the arch of the entablature of the door and moved not, nor spoke any word, but there became stationary and remained. And the door whereupon the shadow rested was, if I remember aright, over against the feet of the young Zoilus enshrouded. But we, the seven there assembled, having seen the shadow as it came out from among the draperies, dared not steadily behold it, but cast down our eyes, and gazed continually into the depths of the mirror of ebony. And at length I, Oinos, speaking some low words, demanded of the shadow its dwelling and its appellation. And the shadow answered, "I am SHADOW, and my dwelling is near to the Catacombs of Ptolemais, and hard by those dim plains of Helusion which border upon the foul Charonian canal." And then did we, the seven, start from our seats in horror, and stand trembling, and shuddering, and aghast: for the tones in the voice of the shadow were not the tones of any one being, but of a multitude of beings, and varying in their cadences from syllable to syllable, fell duskily upon our ears in the well remembered and familiar accents of many thousand departed friends.

Edgar Allan Poe

SILENCE--A FABLE

The mountain pinnacles slumber; valleys, crags, and caves are silent.

"LISTEN to me," said the Demon, as he placed his hand upon my head. "The region of which I speak is a dreary region in Libya, by the borders of the river Zäire. And there is no quiet there, nor silence.

"The waters of the river have a saffron and sickly hue; and they flow not onward to the sea, but palpitate forever and forever beneath the red eye of the sun with a tumultuous and convulsive motion. For many miles on either side of the river's oozy bed is a pale desert of gigantic water-lilies. They sigh one unto the other in that solitude, and stretch towards the heaven their long and ghastly necks, and nod to and fro their everlasting heads. And there is an indistinct murmur which cometh out from among them like the rushing of subterrene water. And they sigh one unto the other.

"But there is a boundary to their realm--the boundary of the dark, horrible, lofty forest. There, like the waves about the Hebrides, the low underwood is agitated continually. But there is no wind throughout the heaven. And the tall primeval trees rock eternally hither and thither with a crashing and mighty sound. And from their high summits, one by one, drop everlasting dews. And at the roots, strange poisonous flowers lie writhing in perturbed slumber. And overhead, with a rustling and loud noise, the gray clouds rush westwardly forever until they roll, a cataract, over the fiery wall of the horizon. But there is no wind throughout the heaven. And by the shores of the river Zäire there is neither quiet nor silence.

"It was night, and the rain fell; and, falling, it was rain, but, having fallen, it was blood. And I stood in the morass among the tall lilies, and the rain fell upon my head--and the lilies sighed one unto the other in the solemnity of their desolation.

"And, all at once, the moon arose through the thin ghastly mist, and was crimson in color. And mine eyes fell upon a huge gray rock which stood by the shore of the river and was lighted by the light of the moon. And the rock was gray and ghastly, and tall,--and the rock was gray. Upon its front were characters engraven in the stones; and I walked through the morass of water-lilies, until I came close unto the shore, that I might read the characters upon the stone. But I could not decipher them. And I was going back into the morass when the moon shone with a fuller red, and I turned and looked again upon the rock and upon the characters;--and the characters were DESOLATION.

"And I looked upwards, and there stood a man upon the summit of the rock; and I hid myself among the water-lilies that I might discover the action of the man. And the man was tall and stately in form, and wrapped up from his shoulders to his feet in the toga of old Rome. And the outlines of his figure were indistinct--but his features were the features of a deity; for the mantle of the night, and of the mist, and of the moon, and of the dew, had left uncovered the features of his face. And his brow was lofty with thought, and his eye wild with care; and in the few furrows upon his cheek, I read the fables of sorrow, and weariness, and disgust with mankind, and a longing after solitude.

"And the man sat upon the rock, and leaned his head upon his hand, and looked out upon the desolation. He looked down into the low unquiet shrubbery, and up into the tall primeval trees, and up higher at the rustling heaven, and into the crimson moon. And I lay close within shelter of the lilies, and observed the actions of the man. And the man trembled in the solitude;--but the night waned, and he sat upon the rock.

"And the man turned his attention from the heaven, and looked out upon the dreary river Zäire, and upon the yellow ghastly waters, and upon the pale legions of the water-lilies. And the man listened to the sighs of the water-lilies, and to the murmur that came up from among them. And I lay close within my covert and observed the actions of the man. And the man trembled in the solitude;--but the night waned, and he sat upon the rock.

"Then I went down into the recesses of the morass, and waded afar in among the wilderness of the lilies, and called unto the hippopotami which dwelt among the fens in the recesses of the morass. And the hippopotami heard my call, and came, with the behemoth, unto the foot of the rock, and roared loudly and fearfully beneath the moon. And I lay close within my covert and observed the actions of the man. And the man trembled in the solitude;--but the night waned, and he sat upon the rock.

"Then I cursed the elements with the curse of tumult; and a frightful tempest gathered in the heaven, where before there had been no wind. And the heaven became livid with the violence of the tempest--and the rain beat upon the head of the man--and the floods of the river came down--and the river was tormented into foam--and the water-lilies shrieked within their beds--and the forest crumbled before the wind--and the thunder rolled--and the lightning fell--and the rock rocked to its foundation. And I lay close within my covert and observed the actions of the man. And the man trembled in the solitude;--but the night waned, and he sat upon the rock.

"Then I grew angry and cursed, with the curse of silence, the river, and the lilies, and the wind, and the forest, and the heaven, and the thunder, and the sighs of the water-lilies. And they became accursed, and were still. And the moon ceased to totter up its pathway to heaven--and the thunder died away--and the lightning did not flash--and the clouds hung motionless--and the waters sunk to their level and remained--and the trees ceased to rock--and the water-lilies sighed no more--and the murmur was heard no longer from among them, nor any shadow of sound throughout the vast illimitable desert. And I looked upon the characters of the rock, and they were changed;--and the characters were SILENCE.

"And mine eyes fell upon the countenance of the man, and his countenance was wan with terror. And, hurriedly, he raised his head from his hand, and stood forth upon the rock and listened. But there was no voice throughout the vast illimitable desert, and the characters upon the rock were SILENCE. And the man shuddered, and turned his face away, and fled afar off, in haste, so that I beheld him no more."

...

Now there are fine tales in the volumes of the Magi--in the iron-bound, melancholy volumes of the Magi. Therein, I say, are glorious histories of the Heaven, and of the Earth, and of the mighty Sea--and of the Genii that overruled the sea, and the earth, and the lofty heaven. There was much lore, too, in the sayings which were said by the sybils; and holy, holy things were heard of old by the dim leaves that trembled around Dodona--but, as Allah liveth, that fable which the demon told me as he sat by my side in the shadow of the tomb, I hold to be the most wonderful of all! And as the Demon made an end of his story, he fell back within the cavity of the tomb and laughed. And I could not laugh with the Demon, and he cursed me because I could not laugh. And the lynx which dwelleth forever in the tomb, came out therefrom, and lay down at the feet of the Demon, and looked at him steadily in the face.

ESSAYS

THE POETIC PRINCIPLE

In speaking of the Poetic Principle, I have no design to be either thorough or profound. While discussing very much at random the essentiality of what we call Poetry, my principal purpose will be to cite for consideration some few of those minor English or American poems which best suit my own taste, or which, upon my own fancy, have left the most definite impression. By "minor poems" I mean, of course, poems of little length. And here, in the beginning, permit me to say a few words in regard to a somewhat peculiar principle, which, whether rightfully or wrongfully, has always had its influence in my own critical estimate of the poem. I hold that a long poem does not exist. I maintain that the phrase, "a long poem," is simply a flat contradiction in terms.

I need scarcely observe that a poem deserves its title only inasmuch as it excites, by elevating the soul. The value of the poem is in the ratio of this elevating excitement. But all excitements are, through a psychal necessity, transient. That degree of excitement which would entitle a poem to be so called at all, cannot be sustained throughout a composition of any great length. After the lapse of half an hour, at the very utmost, it flags--fails--a revulsion ensues-- and then the poem is, in effect, and in fact, no longer such.

There are, no doubt, many who have found difficulty in reconciling the critical dictum that the "Paradise Lost" is to be devoutly admired throughout, with the absolute impossibility of maintaining for it, during perusal, the amount of enthusiasm which that critical dictum would demand. This great work, in fact, is to be regarded as poetical only when, losing sight of that vital requisite in all works of Art, Unity, we view it merely as a series of minor poems. If, to preserve its Unity--its totality of effect or impression--we read it (as would be necessary) at a single sitting, the result is but a constant alternation of excitement and depression. After a passage of what we feel to be true poetry, there follows, inevitably, a passage of platitude which no critical prejudgment can force us to admire; but if, upon completing the work, we read it again; omitting the first book--that is to say, commencing with the second--we shall be surprised at now finding that admirable which we before condemned--that damnable which we had previously so much admired. It follows from all this that the ultimate, aggregate, or absolute effect of even the best epic under the sun, is a nullity--and this is precisely the fact.

In regard to the Iliad, we have, if not positive proof, at least very good reason, for believing it intended as a series of lyrics; but, granting the epic intention, I can say only that the work is based in an imperfect sense of Art. The modern epic is, of the supposititious ancient model, but an inconsiderate and blindfold imitation. But the day of these artistic anomalies is over. If, at any time, any very long poem were popular in reality--which I doubt--it is at least clear that no very long poem will ever be popular again.

That the extent of a poetical work is ceteris paribus, the measure of its merit, seems undoubtedly, when we thus state it, a proposition sufficiently absurd--yet we are indebted for it to the Quarterly Reviews. Surely there can be nothing in mere size, abstractly considered--there can be nothing in mere bulk, so far as a volume is concerned, which has so continuously elicited admiration from these saturnine pamphlets! A mountain, to be sure, by the mere sentiment of physical magnitude which it conveys, does impress us with a sense of the sublime--but no man is impressed after this fashion by the material grandeur of even "The Columbiad." Even the Quarterlies have not instructed us to be so impressed by it. As yet, they have not insisted on our estimating Lamartine by the cubic foot, or Pollock by the pound--but what else are we to infer from their continual prating about "sustained effort"? If, by "sustained effort," any little gentleman has accomplished an epic, let us frankly commend him for the effort--if this indeed be a thing commendable--but let us forbear praising the epic on the effort's account. It is to be hoped thai common sense, in the time to come, will prefer deciding upon a work of Art rather by the impression it makes--by the effect it produces--than by the time it took to impress the effect, or by the amount of "sustained effort" which had been found necessary in effecting the impression. The fact is, that perseverance is one thing and genius quite another--nor can all the Quarterlies in Christendom confound them. By and by, this proposition, with many which I have been just urging, will be received as self-evident. In the meantime, by being generally condemned as falsities, they will not be essentially damaged as truths.

On the other hand, it is clear that a poem may be improperly brief. Undue brevity degenerates into mere epigrammatism. A very short poem, while now and then producing a brilliant or vivid, never produces a profound or enduring effect. There must be the steady pressing down of the stamp upon the wax. De Béranger has wrought innumerable things, pungent and spirit-stirring, but in general they have been too imponderous to stamp themselves deeply into the public attention, and thus, as so many feathers of fancy, have been blown aloft only to be whistled down the wind.

A remarkable instance of the effect of undue brevity in depressing a poem, in keeping it out of the popular view, is afforded by the following exquisite little Serenade:

I arise from dreams of thee
   In the first sweet sleep of night
When the winds are breathing low,
   And the stars are shining bright.
I arise from dreams of thee,
   And a spirit in my feet
Has led me--who knows how?--
   To thy chamber-window, sweet!

The wandering airs they faint
   On the dark the silent stream--
The champak odors fail
   Like sweet thoughts in a dream;

The nightingale's complaint,
    It dies upon her heart,
As I must die on thine,
    O, beloved as thou art!

O, lift me from the grass!
    I die, I faint, I fail!
Let thy love in kisses rain
    On my lips and eyelids pale.
My cheek is cold and white, alas!
    My heart beats loud and fast:
O, press it close to thine again,
    Where it will break at last!

Very few perhaps are familiar with these lines, yet no less a poet than Shelley is their author. Their warm, yet delicate and ethereal imagination will be appreciated by all, but by none so thoroughly as by him who has himself arisen from sweet dreams of one beloved to bathe in the aromatic air of a southern midsummer night.

One of the finest poems by Willis, the very best in my opinion which he has ever written, has no doubt, through this same defect of undue brevity, been kept back from its proper position, not less in the critical than in the popular view:

The shadows lay along Broadway,
    'Twas near the twilight-tide--
And slowly there a lady fair
    Was walking in her pride.
Alone walk'd she; but, viewlessly
    Walk'd spirits at her side.

Peace charm'd the street beneath her feet,
    And honor charm'd the air;
And all astir looked kind on her,
    And called her good as fair--
For all God ever gave to her
    She kept with chary care.

She kept with care her beauties rare
    From lovers warm and true--
For heart was cold to all but gold,
    And the rich came not to woo--
But honor'd well her charms to sell,
    If priests the selling do.

Now walking there was one more fair--
    A slight girl, lily-pale;
And she had unseen company
    To make the spirit quail--
Twixt Want and Scorn she walk'd forlorn,

> And nothing could avail.
>
> No mercy now can clear her brow
>   From this world's peace to pray,
> For as love's wild prayer dissolved in air,
>   Her woman's heart gave way!--
> But the sin forgiven by Christ in Heaven,
>   By man is cursed alway!

    In this composition we find it difficult to recognise the Willis who has written so many mere "verses of society." The lines are not only richly ideal but full of energy, while they breathe an earnestness, an evident sincerity of sentiment, for which we look in vain throughout all the other works of this author.

    While the epic mania, while the idea that to merit in poetry prolixity is indispensable, has for some years past been gradually dying out of the public mind, by mere dint of its own absurdity, we find it succeeded by a heresy too palpably false to be long tolerated, but one which, in the brief period it has already endured, may be said to have accomplished more in the corruption of our Poetical Literature than all its other enemies combined. I allude to the heresy of The Didactic. It has been assumed, tacitly and avowedly, directly and indirectly, that the ultimate object of all Poetry is truth. Every poem, it is said, should inculcate a moral, and by this moral is the poetical merit of the work to be adjudged. We Americans especially have patronized this happy idea, and we Bostonians very especially have developed it in full. We have taken it into our heads that to write a poem simply for the poem's sake, and to acknowledge such to have been our design, would be to confess ourselves radically wanting in the true poetic dignity and force:--but the simple fact is that would we but permit ourselves to look into our own souls we should immediately there discover that under the sun there neither exists nor can exist any work more thoroughly dignified, more supremely noble, than this very poem, this poem per se, this poem which is a poem and nothing more, this poem written solely for the poem's sake.

    With as deep a reverence for the True as ever inspired the bosom of man, I would nevertheless limit, in some measure, its modes of inculcation. I would limit to enforce them. I would not enfeeble them by dissipation. The demands of Truth are severe. She has no sympathy with the myrtles. All that which is so indispensable in Song is precisely all that with which she has nothing whatever to do. It is but making her a flaunting paradox to wreathe her in gems and flowers. In enforcing a truth we need severity rather than efflorescence of language. We must be simple, precise, terse. We must be cool, calm, unimpassioned. In a word, we must be in that mood which, as nearly as possible, is the exact converse of the poetical. He must be blind indeed who does not perceive the radical and chasmal difference between the truthful and the poetical modes of inculcation. He must be theory-mad beyond redemption who, in spite of these differences, shall still persist in attempting to reconcile the obstinate oils and waters of Poetry and Truth.

    Dividing the world of mind into its three most immediately obvious distinctions, we have the Pure Intellect, Taste, and the Moral Sense. I place Taste in the middle because it is just this position which in the mind it occupies.

It holds intimate relations with either extreme; but from the Moral Sense is separated by so faint a difference that Aristotle has not hesitated to place some of its operations among the virtues themselves. Nevertheless we find the offices of the trio marked with a sufficient distinction. Just as the Intellect concerns itself with Truth, so Taste informs us of the Beautiful, while the Moral Sense is regardful of Duty. Of this latter, while Conscience teaches the obligation, and Reason the expediency, Taste contents herself with displaying the charms, waging war upon Vice solely on the ground of her deformity, her disproportion, her animosity to the fitting, to the appropriate, to the harmonious, in a word, to Beauty.

An immortal instinct deep within the spirit of man is thus plainly a sense of the Beautiful. This it is which administers to his delight in the manifold forms, and sounds, and odors, and sentiments amid which he exists. And just as the lily is repeated in the lake, or the eyes of Amaryllis in the mirror, so is the mere oral or written repetition of these forms, and sounds, and colors, and odors, and sentiments a duplicate source of delight. But this mere repetition is not poetry. He who shall simply sing, with however glowing enthusiasm, or with however vivid a truth of description, of the sights, and sounds, and odors, and colors, and sentiments which greet him in common with all mankind--he, I say, has yet failed to prove his divine title. There is still a something in the distance which he has been unable to attain. We have still a thirst unquenchable, to allay which he has not shown us the crystal springs. This thirst belongs to the immortality of man. It is at once a consequence and an indication of his perennial existence. It is the desire of the moth for the star. It is no mere appreciation of the Beauty before us, but a wild effort to reach the Beauty above. Inspired by an ecstatic prescience of the glories beyond the grave, we struggle by multiform combinations among the things and thoughts of Time to attain a portion of that Loveliness whose very elements perhaps appertain to eternity alone. And thus when by Poetry, or when by Music, the most entrancing of the poetic moods, we find ourselves melted into tears, we weep then, not as the Abbate Gravina supposes, through excess of pleasure, but through a certain petulant, impatient sorrow at our inability to grasp now, wholly, here on earth, at once and forever, those divine and rapturous joys of which through the poem, or through the music, we attain to but brief and indeterminate glimpses.

The struggle to apprehend the supernal Loveliness--this struggle, on the part of souls fittingly constituted--has given to the world all that which it (the world) has ever been enabled at once to understand and to feel as poetic.

The Poetic Sentiment, of course, may develop itself in various modes--in Painting, in Sculpture, in Architecture, in the Dance--very especially in Music-- and very peculiarly, and with a wide field, in the composition of the Landscape Garden. Our present theme, however, has regard only to its manifestation in words. And here let me speak briefly on the topic of rhythm. Contenting myself with the certainty that Music, in its various modes of metre, rhythm, and rhyme, is of so vast a moment in Poetry as never to be wisely rejected--is so vitally important an adjunct, that he is simply silly who declines its assistance, I will not now pause to maintain its absolute essentiality. It is in Music perhaps that the soul most nearly attains the great end for which, when inspired by the poetic Sentiment, it struggles--the creation of supernal Beauty. It may be, indeed, that here this sublime end is, now and, then, attained in fact. We are often made to feel, with a shivering delight, that from an earthly harp are stricken notes which cannot have been unfamiliar to the angels. And thus there can be little doubt that in the union of Poetry with Music in its popular sense, we shall find the widest field for the Poetic development. The old Bards and Minnesingers had advantages which we do not possess--and Thomas Moore, singing his own songs, was, in the most legitimate manner, perfecting them as poems.

To recapitulate then:--I would define, in brief, the Poetry of words as The Rhythmical Creation of Beauty. Its sole arbiter is Taste. With the Intellect or with the Conscience it has only collateral relations. Unless incidentally, it has no concern whatever either with Duty or with Truth.

A few words, however, in explanation. That pleasure which is at once the most pure, the most elevating, and the most intense, is derived, I maintain, from the contemplation of the Beautiful. In the contemplation of Beauty we alone find it possible to attain that pleasurable elevation, or excitement of the soul, which we recognize as the Poetic Sentiment, and which is so easily distinguished from Truth, which is the satisfaction of the Reason, or from Passion, which is the excitement of the heart. I make Beauty, therefore--using the word as inclusive of the sublime--I make Beauty the province of the poem, simply because it is an obvious rule of Art that effects should be made to spring as directly as possible from their causes:--no one as yet having been weak enough to deny that the peculiar elevation in question is at least most readily attainable in the poem. It by no means follows, however, that the incitements of Passion, or the precepts of Duty, or even the lessons of Truth, may not be introduced into a poem, and with advantage; for they may subserve incidentally, in various ways, the general purposes of the work: but the true artist will always contrive to tone them down in proper subjection to that Beauty which is the atmosphere and the real essence of the poem.

I cannot better introduce the few poems which I shall present for your consideration, than by the citation of the Pröem to Longfellow's "Waif":

The day is done, and the darkness
    Falls from the wings of Night,
As a feather is wafted downward
    From an eagle in his flight.

I see the lights of the village
    Gleam through the rain and the mist,
And a feeling of sadness comes o'er me,
    That my soul cannot resist;

A feeling of sadness and longing,
    That is not akin to pain,
And resembles sorrow only
    As the mist resembles the rain.

Come, read to me some poem,
    Some simple and heartfelt lay,
That shall soothe this restless feeling,
    And banish the thoughts of day.

Not from the grand old masters,
    Not from the bards sublime,
Whose distant footsteps echo
    Through the corridors of Time.

For, like strains of martial music,
    Their mighty thoughts suggest
Life's endless toil and endeavor;
    And to-night I long for rest.

Read from some humbler poet,
    Whose songs gushed from his heart,
As showers from the clouds of summer,
    Or tears from the eyelids start;

Who through long days of labor,
    And nights devoid of ease,
Still heard in his soul the music
    Of wonderful melodies.

Such songs have power to quiet
    The restless pulse of care,
And come like the benediction
    That follows after prayer.

Then read from the treasured volume
    The poem of thy choice,
And lend to the rhyme of the poet
    The beauty of thy voice.

And the night shall be filled with music,
    And the cares that infest the day,
Shall fold their tents like the Arabs,
    And as silently steal away.

With no great range of imagination, these lines have been justly admired for their delicacy of expression. Some of the images are very effective. Nothing can be better than

    --the bards sublime,
Whose distant footsteps echo
Down the corridors of Time.

The idea of the last quatrain is also very effective. The poem on the whole, however, is chiefly to be admired for the graceful insouciance of its metre, so well in accordance with the character of the sentiments, and especially for the ease of the general manner. This "ease" or naturalness, in a literary style, it has long been the fashion to regard as ease in appearance alone--as a point of really difficult attainment. But not so:--a natural manner is difficult only to him who should never meddle with it--to the unnatural. It is but the result of writing with the understanding, or with the instinct, that the tone, in composition, should always be that which the mass of mankind would adopt--and must perpetually vary, of course, with the occasion. The author who, after the fashion of The North American Review, should be upon all occasions merely "quiet," must necessarily upon many occasions be simply silly, or stupid; and has no more right to be considered "easy" or "natural" than a Cockney exquisite, or than the sleeping Beauty in the waxworks.

Among the minor poems of Bryant, none has so much impressed me as the one which he entitles "June." I quote only a portion of it:

There, through the long, long summer hours,
    The golden light should lie,
And thick young herbs and groups of flowers
    Stand in their beauty by.
The oriole should build and tell
His love-tale, close beside my cell;
    The idle butterfly
Should rest him there, and there be heard
The housewife-bee and humming bird.

And what, if cheerful shouts at noon,
    Come, from the village sent,
Or songs of maids, beneath the moon,
    With fairy laughter blent?
And what if, in the evening light,
Betrothed lovers walk in sight
    Of my low monument?
I would the lovely scene around
Might know no sadder sight nor sound.

I know, I know I should not see
    The season's glorious show,
Nor would its brightness shine for me;
    Nor its wild music flow;

But if, around my place of sleep,
The friends I love should come to weep,
    They might not haste to go.
Soft airs and song, and light and bloom,
Should keep them lingering by my tomb.

These to their soften'd hearts should bear
    The thought of what has been,
And speak of one who cannot share
    The gladness of the scene;
Whose part in all the pomp that fills
The circuit of the summer hills,
    Is--that his grave is green;
And deeply would their hearts rejoice
To hear again his living voice.

The rhythmical flow here is even voluptuous--nothing could be more melodious. The poem has always affected me in a remarkable manner. The intense melancholy which seems to well up, perforce, to the surface of all the poet's cheerful sayings about his grave, we find thrilling us to the soul--while there is the truest poetic elevation in the thrill. The impression left is one of a pleasurable sadness. And if, in the remaining compositions which I shall introduce to you, there be more or less of a similar tone always apparent, let me remind you that (how or why we know not) this certain taint of sadness is inseparably connected with all the higher manifestations of true Beauty. It is, nevertheless,

A feeling of sadness and longing
    That is not akin to pain,
And resembles sorrow only
    As the mist resembles the rain.

The taint of which I speak is clearly perceptible even in a poem so full of brilliancy and spirit as "The Health" of Edward Coote Pinkney:

I fill this cup to one made up
    Of loveliness alone,
A woman, of her gentle sex
    The seeming paragon;
To whom the better elements
    And kindly stars have given
A form so fair, that like the air,
    'Tis less of earth than heaven.

Her every tone is music's own,
    Like those of morning birds,
And something more than melody
    Dwells ever in her words;
The coinage of her heart are they,
    And from her lips each flows
As one may see the burden'd bee
    Forth issue from the rose.

Affections are as thoughts to her,
    The measures of her hours;
Her feelings have the fragrancy,
    The freshness of young flowers;
And lovely passions, changing oft,
    So fill her, she appears
The image of themselves by turns,--
    The idol of past years!

Of her bright face one glance will trace
    A picture on the brain,
And of her voice in echoing hearts
    A sound must long remain;

But memory, such as mine of her,
    So very much endears,
When death is nigh my latest sigh
    Will not be life's, but hers.

I fill'd this cup to one made up
    Of loveliness alone,
A woman, of her gentle sex
    The seeming paragon--
Her health! and would on earth there stood,
    Some more of such a frame,
That life might be all poetry,
    And weariness a name.

    It was the misfortune of Mr. Pinkney to have been born too far south. Had he been a New Englander, it is probable that he would have been ranked as the first of American lyrists by that magnanimous cabal which has so long controlled the destinies of American Letters, in conducting the thing called 'The North American Review'. The poem just cited is especially beautiful; but the poetic elevation which it induces we must refer chiefly to our sympathy in the poet's enthusiasm. We pardon his hyperboles for the evident earnestness with which they are uttered.

    It was by no means my design, however, to expatiate upon the merits of what I should read you. These will necessarily speak for themselves. Boccalina, in his 'Advertisements from Parnassus', tells us that Zoilus once presented Apollo a very caustic criticism upon a very admirable book:--whereupon the god asked him for the beauties of the work. He replied that he only busied himself about the errors. On hearing this, Apollo, handing him a sack of unwinnowed wheat, bade him pick out all the chaff for his reward.

    Now this fable answers very well as a hit at the critics--but I am by no means sure that the god was in the right. I am by no means certain that the true limits of the critical duty are not grossly misunderstood. Excellence, in a poem especially, may be considered in the light of an axiom, which need only be properly put, to become self-evident. It is not excellence if it require to be demonstrated its such:--and thus to point out too particularly the merits of a work of Art, is to admit that they are not merits altogether.

    Among the "Melodies" of Thomas Moore is one whose distinguished character as a poem proper seems to have been singularly left out of view. I allude to his lines beginning--"Come, rest in this bosom." The intense energy of their expression is not surpassed by anything in Byron. There are two of the lines in which a sentiment is conveyed that embodies the all in all of the divine passion of Love--a sentiment which, perhaps, has found its echo in more, and in more passionate, human hearts that any other single sentiment ever embodied in words:

Come, rest in this bosom, my own stricken deer,
Though the herd have fled from thee, thy home is still here;
Here still is the smile, that no cloud can o'ercast,
And a heart and a hand all thy own to the last.

Oh! what was love made for, if 'tis not the same
Through joy and through torment, through glory and shame?
I know not, I ask not, if guilt's in that heart,
I but know that I love thee, whatever thou art.

Thou hast call'd me thy Angel in moments of bliss,
And thy Angel I'll be, 'mid the horrors of this,--
Through the furnace, unshrinking, thy steps to pursue,
And shield thee, and save thee,--or perish there too!

    It has been the fashion of late days to deny Moore Imagination, while granting him Fancy--a distinction originating with Coleridge--than whom no man more fully comprehended the great powers of Moore. The fact is, that the fancy of this poet so far predominates over all his other faculties, and over the fancy of all other men, as to have induced, very naturally, the idea that he is fanciful only. But never was there a greater mistake. Never was a grosser wrong done the fame of a true poet. In the compass of the English language I can call to mind no poem more profoundly--more weirdly imaginative, in the best sense, than the lines commencing--"I would I were by that dim lake"--which are the composition of Thomas Moore. I regret that I am unable to remember them.

    One of the noblest--and, speaking of Fancy--one of the most singularly fanciful of modern poets, was Thomas Hood. His "Fair Ines" had always for me an inexpressible charm:

O saw ye not fair Ines?
    She's gone into the West,
To dazzle when the sun is down
    And rob the world of rest
She took our daylight with her,
    The smiles that we love best,
With morning blushes on her cheek,
    And pearls upon her breast.

O turn again, fair Ines,
    Before the fall of night,
For fear the moon should shine alone,
    And stars unrivall'd bright;
And blessed will the lover be
    That walks beneath their light,
And breathes the love against thy cheek
    I dare not even write!

Would I had been, fair Ines,
    That gallant cavalier,
Who rode so gaily by thy side,
    And whisper'd thee so near!
Were there no bonny dames at home,
    Or no true lovers here,
That he should cross the seas to win

> The dearest of the dear?

I saw thee, lovely Ines,
    Descend along the shore,
With bands of noble gentlemen,
    And banners-waved before;
And gentle youth and maidens gay,
    And snowy plumes they wore;
It would have been a beauteous dream,
    If it had been no more!

Alas, alas, fair Ines,
    She went away with song,
With Music waiting on her steps,
    And shoutings of the throng;
But some were sad and felt no mirth,
    But only Music's wrong,
In sounds that sang Farewell, Farewell,
    To her you've loved so long.

Farewell, farewell, fair Ines,
    That vessel never bore
So fair a lady on its deck,
    Nor danced so light before,--
Alas for pleasure on the sea,
    And sorrow on the shore!
The smile that blest one lover's heart
    Has broken many more!

"The Haunted House," by the same author, is one of the truest poems ever written,--one of the truest, one of the most unexceptionable, one of the most thoroughly artistic, both in its theme and in its execution. It is, moreover, powerfully ideal--imaginative. I regret that its length renders it unsuitable for the purposes of this lecture. In place of it permit me to offer the universally appreciated "Bridge of Sighs:"

One more Unfortunate,
Weary of breath,
Rashly importunate
Gone to her death!

Take her up tenderly,
Lift her with care;--
Fashion'd so slenderly,
Young and so fair!

Look at her garments
Clinging like cerements;
Whilst the wave constantly
Drips from her clothing;

Take her up instantly,
Loving, not loathing.

Touch her not scornfully
Think of her mournfully,
Gently and humanly;
Not of the stains of her,
All that remains of her
Now is pure womanly.

Make no deep scrutiny
Into her mutiny
Rash and undutiful;
Past all dishonor,
Death has left on her
Only the beautiful.

Where the lamps quiver
So far in the river,
With many a light
From window and casement,
From garret to basement,
She stood, with amazement,
Houseless by night.

The bleak wind of March
Made her tremble and shiver;
But not the dark arch,
Or the black flowing river:
Mad from life's history,
Glad to death's mystery,
Swift to be hurl'd--
Anywhere, anywhere
Out of the world!

In she plunged boldly,
No matter how coldly
The rough river ran,--
Over the brink of it,
Picture it,--think of it,
Dissolute Man!
Lave in it, drink of it
Then, if you can!

Still, for all slips of hers,
One of Eve's family--
Wipe those poor lips of hers
Oozing so clammily,
Loop up her tresses
Escaped from the comb,

Edgar Allan Poe

Her fair auburn tresses;
Whilst wonderment guesses
Where was her home?

Who was her father?
Who was her mother!
Had she a sister?
Had she a brother?
Or was there a dearer one
Still, and a nearer one
Yet, than all other?

Alas! for the rarity
Of Christian charity
Under the sun!
Oh! it was pitiful!
Near a whole city full,
Home she had none.

Sisterly, brotherly,
Fatherly, motherly,
Feelings had changed:
Love, by harsh evidence,
Thrown from its eminence;
Even God's providence
Seeming estranged.

Take her up tenderly;
Lift her with care;
Fashion'd so slenderly,
Young, and so fair!
Ere her limbs frigidly
Stiffen too rigidly,
Decently,--kindly,--
Smooth and compose them;
And her eyes, close them,
Staring so blindly!

Dreadfully staring
Through muddy impurity,
As when with the daring
Last look of despairing
Fixed on futurity.

Perishing gloomily,
Spurred by contumely,
Cold inhumanity,
Burning insanity,
Into her rest,--
Cross her hands humbly,

As if praying dumbly,
Over her breast!
Owning her weakness,
Her evil behavior,
And leaving, with meekness,
Her sins to her Saviour!

    The vigor of this poem is no less remarkable than its pathos. The versification, although carrying the fanciful to the very verge of the fantastic, is nevertheless admirably adapted to the wild insanity which is the thesis of the poem.
    Among the minor poems of Lord Byron is one which has never received from the critics the praise which it undoubtedly deserves:

Though the day of my destiny's over,
    And the star of my fate hath declined,
Thy soft heart refused to discover
    The faults which so many could find;
Though thy soul with my grief was acquainted,
    It shrunk not to share it with me,
And the love which my spirit hath painted
    It never hath found but in thee.

Then when nature around me is smiling,
    The last smile which answers to mine,
I do not believe it beguiling,
    Because it reminds me of thine;
And when winds are at war with the ocean,
    As the breasts I believed in with me,
If their billows excite an emotion,
    It is that they bear me from thee.

Though the rock of my last hope is shivered,
    And its fragments are sunk in the wave,
Though I feel that my soul is delivered
    To pain--it shall not be its slave.
There is many a pang to pursue me:
    They may crush, but they shall not contemn--
They may torture, but shall not subdue me--
    'Tis of thee that I think--not of them.

Though human, thou didst not deceive me,
    Though woman, thou didst not forsake,
Though loved, thou forborest to grieve me,
    Though slandered, thou never couldst shake,--
Though trusted, thou didst not disclaim me,
    Though parted, it was not to fly,
Though watchful, 'twas not to defame me,
    Nor mute, that the world might belie.

Yet I blame not the world, nor despise it,
    Nor the war of the many with one--
If my soul was not fitted to prize it,
    'Twas folly not sooner to shun:
And if dearly that error hath cost me,
    And more than I once could foresee,
I have found that whatever it lost me,
    It could not deprive me of thee.

From the wreck of the past, which hath perished,
    Thus much I at least may recall,
It hath taught me that which I most cherished
    Deserved to be dearest of all:
In the desert a fountain is springing,
    In the wide waste there still is a tree,
And a bird in the solitude singing,
    Which speaks to my spirit of thee.

    Although the rhythm here is one of the most difficult, the versification could scarcely be improved. No nobler theme ever engaged the pen of poet. It is the soul-elevating idea that no man can consider himself entitled to complain of Fate while in his adversity he still retains the unwavering love of woman.

    From Alfred Tennyson, although in perfect sincerity I regard him as the noblest poet that ever lived, I have left myself time to cite only a very brief specimen. I call him, and think him the noblest of poets, not because the impressions he produces are at all times the most profound--not because the poetical excitement which he induces is at all times the most intense--but because it is at all times the most ethereal--in other words, the most elevating and most pure. No poet is so little of the earth, earthy. What I am about to read is from his last long poem, "The Princess:"

    Tears, idle tears, I know not what they mean,
Tears from the depth of some divine despair
Rise in the heart, and gather to the eyes,
In looking on the happy Autumn fields,
And thinking of the days that are no more.

    Fresh as the first beam glittering on a sail,
That brings our friends up from the underworld,
Sad as the last which reddens over one
That sinks with all we love below the verge;
So sad, so fresh, the days that are no more.

    Ah, sad and strange as in dark summer dawns
The earliest pipe of half-awaken'd birds
To dying ears, when unto dying eyes
The casement slowly grows a glimmering square;
So sad, so strange, the days that are no more.

    Dear as remember'd kisses after death,

*And sweet as those by hopeless fancy feign'd
On lips that are for others; deep as love,
Deep as first love, and wild with all regret;
O Death in Life, the days that are no more.*

    Thus, although in a very cursory and imperfect manner, I have endeavored to convey to you my conception of the Poetic Principle. It has been my purpose to suggest that, while this Principle itself is strictly and simply the Human Aspiration for Supernal Beauty, the manifestation of the Principle is always found in an elevating excitement of the soul, quite independent of that passion which is the intoxication of the Heart, or of that truth which is the satisfaction of the Reason. For in regard to passion, alas! its tendency is to degrade rather than to elevate the Soul. Love, on the contrary--Love--the true, the divine Eros--the Uranian as distinguished from the Dionasan Venus--is unquestionably the purest and truest of all poetical themes. And in regard to Truth, if, to be sure, through the attainment of a truth we are led to perceive a harmony where none was apparent before, we experience at once the true poetical effect; but this effect is referable to the harmony alone, and not in the least degree to the truth which merely served to render the harmony manifest.

    We shall reach, however, more immediately a distinct conception of what true Poetry is, by mere reference to a few of the simple elements which induce in the Poet himself the true poetical effect. He recognizes the ambrosia which nourishes his soul in the bright orbs that shine in Heaven, in the volutes of the flower, in the clustering of low shrubberies, in the waving of the grain-fields, in the slanting of tall eastern trees, in the blue distance of mountains, in the grouping of clouds, in the twinkling of half-hidden brooks, in the gleaming of silver rivers, in the repose of sequestered lakes, in the star-mirroring depths of lonely wells. He perceives it in the songs of birds, in the harp of Æolus, in the sighing of the night-wind, in the repining voice of the forest, in the surf that complains to the shore, in the fresh breath of the woods, in the scent of the violet, in the voluptuous perfume of the hyacinth, in the suggestive odor that comes to him at eventide from far-distant undiscovered islands, over dim oceans, illimitable and unexplored. He owns it in all noble thoughts, in all unworldly motives, in all holy impulses, in all chivalrous, generous, and self-sacrificing deeds. He feels it in the beauty of woman, in the grace of her step, in the lustre of her eye, in the melody of her voice, in her soft laughter, in her sigh, in the harmony of the rustling of her robes. He deeply feels it in her winning endearments, in her burning enthusiasms, in her gentle charities, in her meek and devotional endurance, but above all, ah, far above all, he kneels to it, he worships it in the faith, in the purity, in the strength, in the altogether divine majesty of her love.

    Let me conclude by the recitation of yet another brief poem, one very different in character from any that I have before quoted. It is by Motherwell, and is called "The Song of the Cavalier." With our modern and altogether rational ideas of the absurdity and impiety of warfare, we are not precisely in that frame of mind best adapted to sympathize with the sentiments, and thus to appreciate the real excellence of the poem. To do this fully we must identify ourselves in fancy with the soul of the old cavalier:

Edgar Allan Poe

A steed! a steed! of matchless speede!
    A sword of metal keene!
Al else to noble heartes is drosse--
    Al else on earth is meane.
The neighynge of the war-horse prowde.
    The rowleing of the drum,
The clangor of the trumpet lowde--
    Be soundes from heaven that come.
And oh! the thundering presse of knightes,
    When as their war-cryes welle,
May tole from heaven an angel bright,
    And rowse a fiend from hell,

Then mounte! then mounte, brave gallants all,
    And don your helmes amaine,
Deathe's couriers, Fame and Honor, call
    Us to the field againe.
No shrewish teares shall fill your eye
    When the sword-hilt's in our hand,--
Heart-whole we'll part, and no whit sighe
    For the fayrest of the land;
Let piping swaine, and craven wight,
    Thus weepe and puling crye,
Our business is like men to fight,
    And hero-like to die!

THE PHILOSOPHY OF COMPOSITION

Charles Dickens, in a note now lying before me, alluding to an examination I once made of the mechanism of Barnaby Rudge, says--"By the way, are you aware that Godwin wrote his Caleb Williams backwards? He first involved his hero in a web of difficulties, forming the second volume, and then, for the first, cast about him for some mode of accounting for what had been done."

I cannot think this the precise mode of procedure on the part of Godwin-- and indeed what he himself acknowledges is not altogether in accordance with Mr. Dickens's idea--but the author of Caleb Williams was too good an artist not to perceive the advantage derivable from at least a somewhat similar process. Nothing is more clear than that every plot, worth the name, must be elaborated to its dénouement before anything be attempted with the pen. It is only with the dénouement constantly in view that we can give a plot its indispensable air of consequence, or causation, by making the incidents, and especially the tone at all points, tend to the development of the intention.

There is a radical error, I think, in the usual mode of constructing a story. Either history affords a thesis--or one is suggested by an incident of the day--or, at best, the author sets himself to work in the combination of striking events to form merely the basis of his narrative---designing, generally, to fill in with description, dialogue, or autorial comment, whatever crevices of fact or action may, from page to page, render themselves apparent.

I prefer commencing with the consideration of an effect. Keeping originality always in view--for he is false to himself who ventures to dispense with so obvious and so easily attainable a source of interest--I say to myself, in the first place, "Of the innumerable effects or impressions of which the heart, the intellect, or (more generally) the soul is susceptible, what one shall I, on the present occasion, select?" Having chosen a novel first, and secondly, a vivid effect, I consider whether it can be best wrought by incident or tone--whether by ordinary incidents and peculiar tone, or the converse, or by peculiarity both of incident and tone--afterwards looking about me (or rather within) for such combinations of events or tone as shall best aid me in the construction of the effect.

I have often thought how interesting a magazine paper might be written by any author who would--that is to say, who could--detail, step by step, the processes by which any one of his compositions attained its ultimate point of completion. Why such a paper has never been given to the world, I am much at a loss to say--but perhaps the autorial vanity has had more to do with the omission than any one other cause. Most writers--poets in especial--prefer having it understood that they compose by a species of fine frenzy--an ecstatic intuition--and would positively shudder at letting the public take a peep behind the scenes, at the elaborate and vacillating crudities of thought--at the true purposes seized only at the last moment--at the innumerable glimpses of idea that arrived not at the maturity of full view--at the fully-matured fancies discarded in despair as unmanageable--at the cautious selections and rejections--at the painful erasures and interpolations,--in a word, at the wheels and pinions, the tackle for scene-shifting, the step-ladders and demon-traps, the cock's feathers, the red paint, and the black patches, which, in ninety-nine cases out of the hundred, constitute the properties of the literary histrio.

I am aware, on the other hand, that the case is by no means common, in which an author is at all in condition to retrace the steps by which his conclusions have been attained. In general, suggestions, having arisen pell-mell, are pursued and forgotten in a similar manner.

For my own part, I have neither sympathy with the repugnance alluded to, nor, at any time, the least difficulty in recalling to mind the progressive steps of any of my compositions; and, since the interest of an analysis, or reconstruction, such as I have considered a desideratum, is quite independent of any real or fancied interest in the thing analyzed, it will not be regarded as a breach of decorum on my part to show the modus operandi by which some one of my own works was put together. I select "The Raven" as most generally known. It is my design to render it manifest that no one point in its composition is referrible either to accident or intuition--that the work proceeded, step by step, to its completion with the precision and rigid consequence of a mathematical problem.

Let us dismiss, as irrelevant to the poem, per se, the circumstance--or say the necessity--which, in the first place, gave rise to the intention of composing a poem that should suit at once the popular and the critical taste.

We commence, then, with this intention.

The initial consideration was that of extent. If any literary work is too long to be read at one sitting, we must be content to dispense with the immensely important effect derivable from unity of impression--for, if two sittings be required, the affairs of the world interfere, and everything like totality is at once destroyed. But since, ceteris paribus, no poet can afford to dispense with anything that may advance his design, it but remains to be seen whether there is, in extent, any advantage to counterbalance the loss of unity which attends it. Here I say no, at once. What we term a long poem is, in fact, merely a succession of brief ones--that is to say, of brief poetical effects. It is needless to demonstrate that a poem is such only inasmuch as it intensely excites, by elevating the soul; and all intense excitements are, through a psychal necessity, brief. For this reason, at least one-half of the "Paradise Lost" is essentially prose--a succession of poetical excitements interspersed, inevitably, with corresponding depressions--the whole being deprived, through the extremeness of its length, of the vastly important artistic element, totality, or unity of effect.

It appears evident, then, that there is a distinct limit, as regards length, to all works of literary art--the limit of a single sitting--and that, although in certain classes of prose composition, such as Robinson Crusoe (demanding no unity), this limit may be advantageously overpassed, it can never properly be overpassed in a poem. Within this limit, the extent of a poem may be made to bear mathematical relation to its merit--in other words, to the excitement or elevation--again, in other words, to the degree of the true poetical effect which it is capable of inducing; for it is clear that the brevity must be in direct ratio of the intensity of the intended effect--this, with one proviso--that a certain degree of duration is absolutely requisite for the production of any effect at all.

Holding in view these considerations, as well as that degree of excitement which I deemed not above the popular, while not below the critical taste, I reached at once what I conceived the proper length for my intended poem--a length of about one hundred lines. It is, in fact, a hundred and eight.

My next thought concerned the choice of an impression, or effect, to be conveyed: and here I may as well observe that, throughout the construction, I kept steadily in view the design of rendering the work universally appreciable. I should be carried too far out of my immediate topic were I to demonstrate a point upon which I have repeatedly insisted, and which, with the poetical, stands not in the slightest need of demonstration--the point, I mean, that Beauty is the sole legitimate province of the poem. A few words, however, in elucidation of my real meaning, which some of my friends have evinced a disposition to misrepresent. That pleasure which is at once the most intense, the most elevating, and the most pure, is, I believe, found in the contemplation of the beautiful. When, indeed, men speak of Beauty, they mean, precisely, not a quality, as is supposed, but an effect--they refer, in short, just to that intense and pure elevation of soul --not of intellect, or of heart--upon which I have commented, and which is experienced in consequence of contemplating "the beautiful." Now I designate Beauty as the province of the poem, merely because it is an obvious rule of Art that effects should be made to spring from direct causes--that objects should be attained through means best adapted for their attainment--no one as yet having been weak enough to deny that the peculiar elevation alluded to is most readily attained in the poem. Now the object Truth, or the satisfaction of the intellect, and the object Passion, or the excitement of the heart, are, although attainable to a certain extent in poetry, far more readily attainable in prose. Truth, in fact, demands a precision, and Passion a homeliness (the truly passionate will comprehend me) which are absolutely antagonistic to that Beauty which, I maintain, is the excitement, or pleasurable elevation, of the soul. It by no means follows from anything here said that passion, or even truth, may not be introduced, and even profitably introduced, into a poem--for they may serve in elucidation, or aid the general effect, as do discords in music, by contrast--but the true artist will always contrive, first, to tone them into proper subservience to the predominant aim, and secondly, to enveil them, as far as possible, in that Beauty which is the atmosphere and the essence of the poem.

Regarding, then, Beauty as my province, my next question referred to the tone of its highest manifestation--and all experience has shown that this tone is one of sadness. Beauty of whatever kind, in its supreme development, invariably excites the sensitive soul to tears. Melancholy is thus the most legitimate of all the poetical tones.

The length, the province, and the tone being thus determined, I betook myself to ordinary induction, with the view of obtaining some artistic piquancy which might serve me as a key-note in the construction of the poem--some pivot upon which the whole structure might turn. In carefully thinking over all the usual artistic effects--or more properly points, in the theatrical sense--I did not fail to perceive immediately that no one had been so universally employed as that of the refrain. The universality of its employment sufficed to assure me of its intrinsic value, and spared me the necessity of submitting it to analysis. I considered it, however, with regard to its susceptibility of improvement, and soon saw it to be in a primitive condition. As commonly used, the refrain, or burden, not only is limited to lyric verse, but depends for its impression upon the force of monotone--both in sound and thought. The pleasure is deduced solely from the sense of identity--of repetition. I resolved to diversify, and so heighten the effect, by adhering in general to the monotone of sound, while I continually varied that of thought: that is to say, I determined to produce continuously novel effects, by the variation of the application of the refrain--the refrain itself remaining, for the most part, unvaried.

These points being settled, I next bethought me of the nature of my refrain. Since its application was to be repeatedly varied, it was clear that the refrain itself must be brief, for there would have been an insurmountable difficulty in frequent variations of application in any sentence of length. In proportion to the brevity of the sentence would of course be the facility of the variation. This led me at once to a single word as the best refrain.

The question now arose as to the character of the word. Having made up my mind to a refrain, the division of the poem into stanzas was of course a corollary, the refrain forming the close to each stanza. That such a close, to have force, must be sonorous and susceptible of protracted emphasis, admitted no doubt, and these considerations inevitably led me to the long o as the most sonorous vowel in connection with r as the most producible consonant.

The sound of the refrain being thus determined, it became necessary to select a word embodying this sound, and at the same time in the fullest possible keeping with that melancholy which I had predetermined as the tone of the poem. In such a search it would have been absolutely impossible to overlook the word "Nevermore." In fact, it was the very first which presented itself.

The next desideratum was a pretext for the continuous use of the one word "nevermore." In observing the difficulty which I at once found in inventing a sufficiently plausible reason for its continuous repetition, I did not fail to perceive that this difficulty arose solely from the pre-assumption that the word was to be so continuously or monotonously spoken by a human being--I did not fail to perceive, in short, that the difficulty lay in the reconciliation of this monotony with the exercise of reason on the part of the creature repeating the word. Here, then, immediately arose the idea of a non-reasoning creature capable of speech; and very naturally, a parrot, in the first instance, suggested itself, but was superseded forthwith by a Raven as equally capable of speech, and infinitely more in keeping with the intended tone.

I had now gone so far as the conception of a Raven, the bird of ill-omen, monotonously repeating the one word "Nevermore" at the conclusion of each stanza in a poem of melancholy tone, and in length about one hundred lines. Now, never losing sight of the object supremeness or perfection at all points, I asked myself--"Of all melancholy topics what, according to the universal understanding of mankind, is the most melancholy?" Death, was the obvious reply. "And when," I said, "is this most melancholy of topics most poetical?" From what I have already explained at some length, the answer here also is obvious--"When it most closely allies itself to Beauty; the death, then, of a beautiful woman is unquestionably the most poetical topic in the world, and equally is it beyond doubt that the lips best suited for such topic are those of a bereaved lover."

I had now to combine the two ideas of a lover lamenting his deceased mistress and a Raven continuously repeating the word "Nevermore." I had to combine these, bearing in mind my design of varying at every turn the application of the word repeated, but the only intelligible mode of such combination is that of imagining the Raven employing the word in answer to the queries of the lover. And here it was that I saw at once the opportunity afforded for the effect on which I had been depending, that is to say, the effect of the variation of application. I saw that I could make the first query propounded by the lover--the first query to which the Raven should reply "Nevermore"--that I could make this first query a commonplace one, the second less so, the third still less, and so on, until at length the lover, startled from his original nonchalance by the melancholy character of the word itself, by its frequent repetition, and by a consideration of the ominous reputation of the fowl that uttered it, is at length excited to superstition, and wildly propounds queries of a far different character--queries whose solution he has passionately at heart--propounds them half in superstition and half in that species of despair which delights in self-torture--propounds them not altogether because he believes in the prophetic or demoniac character of the bird (which reason assures him is merely repeating a lesson learned by rote), but because he experiences a frenzied pleasure in so modelling his questions as to receive from the expected "Nevermore" the most delicious because the most intolerable of sorrow. Perceiving the opportunity thus afforded me, or, more strictly, thus forced upon me in the progress of the construction, I first established in mind the climax or concluding query--that query to which "Nevermore" should be in the last place an answer--that query in reply to which this word "Nevermore" should involve the utmost conceivable amount of sorrow and despair.

Here then the poem may be said to have its beginning, at the end where all works of art should begin; for it was here at this point of my preconsiderations that I first put pen to paper in the composition of the stanza:

"Prophet," said I, "thing of evil! prophet still if bird or devil!
By that heaven that bends above us--by that God we both adore,
Tell this soul with sorrow laden, if within the distant Aidenn,
It shall clasp a sainted maiden whom the angels name Lenore--
Clasp a rare and radiant maiden whom the angels name Lenore."
    Quoth the Raven, "Nevermore."

I composed this stanza, at this point, first that, by establishing the climax, I might the better vary and graduate, as regards seriousness, and importance the preceding queries of the lover, and secondly, that I might definitely settle the rhythm, the metre, and the length and general arrangement of the stanza, as well as graduate the stanzas which were to precede, so that none of them might surpass this in rhythmical effect. Had I been able in the subsequent composition to construct more vigorous stanzas, I should without scruple have purposely enfeebled them so as not to interfere with the climacteric effect.

And here I may as well say a few words of the versification. My first object (as usual) was originality. The extent to which this has been neglected in versification is one of the most unaccountable things in the world. Admitting that there is little possibility of variety in mere rhythm, it is still clear that the possible varieties of metre and stanza are absolutely infinite; and yet, for centuries, no man, in verse has ever done, or ever seemed to think of doing, an original thing. The fact is that originality (unless in minds of very unusual force) is by no means a matter, as some suppose, of impulse or intuition. In general, to be found, it must be elaborately sought and, although a positive merit of the highest class, demands in its attainment less of invention than negation.

Of course I pretend to no originality in either the rhythm or metre of the "Raven." The former is trochaic--the latter is octametre acatalectic, alternating with heptametre catalectic repeated in the refrain of the fifth verse, and terminating with tetrametre catalectic. Less pedantically, the feet employed throughout (trochees) consists of a long syllable followed by a short; the first line of the stanza consists of eight of these feet, the second of seven and a half (in effect two-thirds), the third of eight, the fourth of seven and a half, the fifth the same, the sixth three and a half. Now, each of these lines taken individually has been employed before, and what originality the "Raven" has, is in their combinations into stanzas; nothing even remotely approaching this combination has ever been attempted. The effect of this originality of combination is aided by other unusual and some altogether novel effects, arising from an extension of the application of the principles of rhyme and alliteration.

The next point to be considered was the mode of bringing together the lover and the Raven--and the first branch of this consideration was the locale. For this the most natural suggestion might seem to be a forest, or the fields--but it has always appeared to me that a close circumscription of space is absolutely necessary to the effect of insulated incident--it has the force of a frame to a picture. It has an indisputable moral power in keeping concentrated the attention, and, of course, must not be confounded with mere unity of place.

I determined, then, to place the lover in his chamber--in a chamber rendered sacred to him by memories of her who had frequented it. The room is represented as richly furnished--this in mere pursuance of the ideas I have already explained on the subject of Beauty, as the sole true poetical thesis.

The locale being thus determined, I had now to introduce the bird--and the thought of introducing him through the window was inevitable. The idea of making the lover suppose, in the first instance, that the flapping of the wings of the bird against the shutter, is a "tapping" at the door, originated in a wish to increase, by prolonging, the reader's curiosity, and in a desire to admit the incidental effect arising from the lover's throwing open the door, finding all dark, and thence adopting the half-fancy that it was the spirit of his mistress that knocked.

I made the night tempestuous, first to account for the Raven's seeking admission, and secondly, for the effect of contrast with the (physical) serenity within the chamber.

I made the bird alight on the bust of Pallas, also for the effect of contrast between the marble and the plumage--it being understood that the bust was absolutely suggested by the bird--the bust of Pallas being chosen, first, as most in keeping with the scholarship of the lover, and, secondly, for the sonorousness of the word, Pallas, itself.

About the middle of the poem, also, I have availed myself of the force of contrast, with a view of deepening the ultimate impression. For example, an air of the fantastic--approaching as nearly to the ludicrous as was admissible--is given to the Raven's entrance. He comes in "with many a flirt and flutter."

Not the least obeisance made he--not a moment stopped or stayed he,
But with mien of lord or lady, perched above my chamber door.

In the two stanzas which follow, the design is more obviously carried out:

Then this ebony bird beguiling my sad fancy into smiling
By the grave and stern decorum of the countenance it wore,
"Though thy crest be shorn and shaven, thou," I said, "art sure no craven,
Ghastly grim and ancient Raven wandering from the nightly shore--
Tell me what thy lordly name is on the night's Plutonian shore?"
    Quoth the Raven, "Nevermore."

Much I marvelled this ungainly fowl to hear discourse so plainly,
Though its answer little meaning--little relevancy bore;
For we cannot help agreeing that no living human being
Ever yet was blessed with seeing bird above his chamber door--
Bird or beast upon the sculptured bust above his chamber door,
    With such name as "Nevermore."

The effect of the dénouement being thus provided for, I immediately drop the fantastic for a tone of the most profound seriousness--this tone commencing in the stanza directly following the one last quoted, with the line,

But the Raven, sitting lonely on that placid bust, spoke only, etc.

From this epoch the lover no longer jests--no longer sees anything even of the fantastic in the Raven's demeanor. He speaks of him as a "grim, ungainly, ghastly, gaunt, and ominous bird of yore," and feels the "fiery eyes" burning into his "bosom's core." This revolution of thought, or fancy, on the lover's part, is intended to induce a similar one on the part of the reader--to bring the mind into a proper frame for the dénouement--which is now brought about as rapidly and as directly as possible.

With the dénouement proper--with the Raven's reply, "Nevermore," to the lover's final demand if he shall meet his mistress in another world--the poem, in its obvious phase, that of a simple narrative, may be said to have its completion. So far, everything is within the limits of the accountable--of the real. A raven having learned by rote the single word "Nevermore," and having escaped from the custody of its owner, is driven at midnight, through the violence of a storm, to seek admission at a window from which a light still gleams--the chamber-window of a student, occupied half in pouring over a volume, half in dreaming of a beloved mistress deceased. The casement being thrown open at the fluttering of the bird's wings, the bird itself perches on the most convenient seat out of the immediate reach of the student, who, amused by the incident and the oddity of the visitor's demeanor, demands of it, in jest and with out looking for a reply, its name. The Raven addressed, answers with its customary word, "Nevermore"--a word which finds immediate echo in the melancholy heart of the student, who, giving utterance aloud to certain thoughts suggested by the occasion, is again startled by the fowl's repetition of "Nevermore." The student now guesses the state of the case, but is impelled, as I have before explained, by the human thirst for self-torture, and in part by superstition, to propound such queries to the bird as will bring him, the lover, the most of the luxury of sorrow through the anticipated answer "Nevermore." With the indulgence, to the extreme, of this self-torture, the narration, in what I have termed its first or obvious phase, has a natural termination, and so far there has been no overstepping of the limits of the real.

But in subjects so handled, however skilfully, or with however vivid an array of incident, there is always a certain hardness or nakedness which repels the artistical eye. Two things are invariably required--first, some amount of complexity, or more properly, adaptation; and, secondly, some amount of suggestiveness, some undercurrent, however indefinite of meaning. It is this latter, in especial, which imparts to a work of art so much of that richness (to borrow from colloquy a forcible term) which we are too fond of confounding with the ideal. It is the excess of the suggested meaning--it is the rendering this the upper instead of the under current of theme--which turns into prose (and that of the very flattest kind) the so-called poetry of the so-called transcendentalists.

Holding these opinions, I added the two concluding stanzas of the poem--their suggestiveness being thus made to pervade all the narrative which has preceded them. The undercurrent of meaning is rendered first apparent in the lines:

"Take thy beak from out my heart, and take thy form from off my door!"
    Quoth the Raven, "Nevermore!"

It will be observed that the words, "from out my heart," involve the first metaphorical expression in the poem. They, with the answer, "Nevermore," dispose the mind to seek a moral in all that has been previously narrated. The reader begins now to regard the Raven as emblematical--but it is not until the very last line of the very last stanza, that the intention of making him emblematical of Mournful and never-ending Remembrance is permitted distinctly to be seen:

And the Raven, never flitting, still is sitting, still is sitting
On the pallid bust of Pallas just above my chamber door;
And his eyes have all the seeming of a demon's that is dreaming,
And the lamplight o'er him streaming throws his shadow on the floor;
And my soul from out that shadow that lies floating on the floor
    Shall be lifted--nevermore!

OLD ENGLISH POETRY [1]

It should not be doubted that at least one-third of the affection with which we regard the elder poets of Great Britain should be attributed to what is, in itself, a thing apart from poetry--we mean to the simple love of the antique--and that, again, a third of even the proper poetic sentiment inspired by their writings, should be ascribed to a fact which, while it has strict connection with poetry in the abstract, and with the old British poems themselves, should not be looked upon as a merit appertaining to the authors of the poems. Almost every devout admirer of the old bards, if demanded his opinion of their productions, would mention vaguely, yet with perfect sincerity, a sense of dreamy, wild, indefinite, and he would perhaps say, indefinable delight; on being required to point out the source of this so shadowy pleasure, he would be apt to speak of the quaint in phraseology and in general handling. This quaintness is, in fact, a very powerful adjunct to ideality, but in the case in question it arises independently of the author's will, and is altogether apart from his intention. Words and their rhythm have varied. Verses which affect us to-day with a vivid delight, and which delight, in many instances, may be traced to the one source, quaintness, must have worn in the days of their construction a very commonplace air. This is, of course, no argument against the poems now--we mean it only as against the poets then. There is a growing desire to overrate them. The old English muse was frank, guileless, sincere and although very learned, still learned without art. No general error evinces a more thorough confusion of ideas than the error of supposing Donne and Cowley metaphysical in the sense wherein Wordsworth and Coleridge are so. With the two former ethics were the end--with the two latter the means. The poet of the "Creation" wished, by highly artificial verse, to inculcate what he supposed to be moral truth--the poet of the "Ancient Mariner" to infuse the Poetic Sentiment through channels suggested by analysis. The one finished by complete failure what he commenced in the grossest misconception; the other, by a path which could not possibly lead him astray, arrived at a triumph which is not the less glorious because hidden from the profane eyes of the multitude. But in this view even the "metaphysical verse" of Cowley is but evidence of the simplicity and single-heartedness of the man. And he was in this but a type of his school--for we may as well designate in this way the entire class of writers whose poems are bound up in the volume before us, and throughout all of whom there runs a very perceptible general character. They used little art in composition. Their writings sprang immediately from the soul--and partook intensely of that soul's nature. Nor is it difficult to perceive the tendency of this abandon--to elevate immeasurably all the energies of mind--but, again, so to mingle the greatest possible fire, force, delicacy, and all good things, with the lowest possible bathos, baldness, and imbecility, as to render it not a matter of doubt that the average results of mind in such a school will be found inferior to those results in one (ceteris paribus) more artificial.

Edgar Allan Poe

    We cannot bring ourselves to believe that the selections of the "Book of Gems" are such as will impart to a poetical reader the clearest possible idea of the beauty of the school--but if the intention had been merely to show the school's character, the attempt might have been considered successful in the highest degree. There are long passages now before us of the most despicable trash, with no merit whatever beyond that of their antiquity. The criticisms of the editor do not particularly please us. His enthusiasm is too general and too vivid not to be false. His opinion, for example, of Sir Henry's Wotton's "Verses on the Queen of Bohemia"--that "there are few finer things in our language," is untenable and absurd.

    In such lines we can perceive not one of those higher attributes of Poesy which belong to her in all circumstances and throughout all time. Here everything is art, nakedly, or but awkwardly concealed. No prepossession for the mere antique (and in this case we can imagine no other prepossession) should induce us to dignify with the sacred name of poetry, a series, such as this, of elaborate and threadbare compliments, stitched, apparently, together, without fancy, without plausibility, and without even an attempt at adaptation.

    In common with all the world, we have been much delighted with "The Shepherd's Hunting" by Withers--a poem partaking, in a remarkable degree, of the peculiarities of 'Il Penseroso'. Speaking of Poesy, the author says:

"By the murmur of a spring,
Or the least boughs rustleling,
By a daisy whose leaves spread,
Shut when Titan goes to bed,
Or a shady bush or tree,
She could more infuse in me
Than all Nature's beauties con
In some other wiser man.
By her help I also now
Make this churlish place allow
Something that may sweeten gladness
In the very gall of sadness--
The dull loneness, the black shade,
That these hanging vaults have made
The strange music of the waves
Beating on these hollow caves,
This black den which rocks emboss,
Overgrown with eldest moss,
The rude portals that give light
More to terror than delight,
This my chamber of neglect
Walled about with disrespect;
From all these and this dull air
A fit object for despair,
She hath taught me by her might
To draw comfort and delight."

But these lines, however good, do not bear with them much of the general character of the English antique. Something more of this will be found in Corbet's "Farewell to the Fairies!" We copy a portion of Marvell's "Maiden lamenting for her Fawn," which we prefer--not only as a specimen of the elder poets, but in itself as a beautiful poem, abounding in pathos, exquisitely delicate imagination and truthfulness--to anything of its species:

"It is a wondrous thing how fleet
'Twas on those little silver feet,
With what a pretty skipping grace
It oft would challenge me the race,
And when't had left me far away
'Twould stay, and run again, and stay;
For it was nimbler much than hinds,
And trod as if on the four winds.
I have a garden of my own,
But so with roses overgrown,
And lilies, that you would it guess
To be a little wilderness;
And all the spring-time of the year
It only loved to be there.
Among the beds of lilies I
Have sought it oft where it should lie,
Yet could not, till itself would rise,
Find it, although before mine eyes.
For in the flaxen lilies shade
It like a bank of lilies laid;
Upon the roses it would feed
Until its lips even seemed to bleed,
And then to me 'twould boldly trip,
And print those roses on my lip,
But all its chief delight was still
With roses thus itself to fill,
And its pure virgin limbs to fold
In whitest sheets of lilies cold,
Had it lived long, it would have been
Lilies without, roses within."

How truthful an air of lamentations hangs here upon every syllable! It pervades all. It comes over the sweet melody of the words--over the gentleness and grace which we fancy in the little maiden herself--even over the half-playful, half-petulant air with which she lingers on the beauties and good qualities of her favorite--like the cool shadow of a summer cloud over a bed of lilies and violets, "and all sweet flowers." The whole is redolent with poetry of a very lofty order. Every line is an idea conveying either the beauty and playfulness of the fawn, or the artlessness of the maiden, or her love, or her admiration, or her grief, or the fragrance and warmth and appropriateness of the little nest-like bed of lilies and roses which the fawn devoured as it lay upon them, and could scarcely be distinguished from them by the once happy little damsel who went to seek her pet with an arch and rosy smile on her face.

Consider the great variety of truthful and delicate thought in the few lines we have quoted--the wonder of the little maiden at the fleetness of her favorite--the "little silver feet"--the fawn challenging his mistress to a race with "a pretty skipping grace," running on before, and then, with head turned back, awaiting her approach only to fly from it again--can we not distinctly perceive all these things? How exceedingly vigorous, too, is the line,

"And trod as if on the four winds!"

a vigor apparent only when we keep in mind the artless character of the speaker and the four feet of the favorite, one for each wind. Then consider the garden of "my own," so overgrown, entangled with roses and lilies, as to be "a little wilderness"--the fawn loving to be there, and there "only"--the maiden seeking it "where it should lie"--and not being able to distinguish it from the flowers until "itself would rise"--the lying among the lilies "like a bank of lilies"--the loving to "fill itself with roses,"

"And its pure virgin limbs to fold
In whitest sheets of lilies cold,"

and these things being its "chief" delights--and then the pre-eminent beauty and naturalness of the concluding lines, whose very hyperbole only renders them more true to nature when we consider the innocence, the artlessness, the enthusiasm, the passionate girl, and more passionate admiration of the bereaved child:

"Had it lived long, it would have been
Lilies without, roses within."

Footnotes:

1. "The Book of Gems." Edited by S. C. Hall.

www.ingramcontent.com/pod-product-compliance
Lightning Source LLC
Chambersburg PA
CBHW030139170426
43199CB00008B/131